Contents

Executive Summary

Land value capture (LVC) is a proven, effective means to finance municipal infrastructure, improvements, and programs. Widely used in Latin America, it is receiving significant attention from policy makers, citizens, the business community, and scholars in the United States as well.

A longstanding mandatory inclusionary housing ordinance in San Jose, California, has withstood court challenges to ensure affordable housing remains available, even as the city expands its suburban residences. *Source: SpVVK/iStock/Getty Images Plus*

Land Value Capture, Explained in Video

Public infrastructure makes community possible. From electricity and water services to roads and sidewalks, almost everything we consume relies on this greater public good. But the public sector constantly struggles to pay for such essential features. More and more, municipalities worldwide are applying land value capture approaches to fund investments. But how do these tools work?

The Lincoln Institute of Land Policy's 10-minute explainer video defines land value capture and illustrates how communities can recover land value increases that result from public action. It provides examples from the "toolbox" of available instruments and shows how communities have used land value capture to promote social equity and finance affordable housing, infrastructure, and other public goods.

To watch the video and learn more, visit lincolninst.edu/lvc-explained.

Also known as land value return, LVC enables communities to recover and reinvest land value increases resulting from public investment and other government actions. As new subway lines, roads, and other public works raise the value of nearby land and real estate, for example, developers and property owners share that publicly generated windfall to help local governments pay for new bridges, transit, parks, affordable housing, and other infrastructure upgrades. Municipalities can also recover some or all of the land value increases that changes to zoning or other regulations might create.

This report examines various land value capture tools that governments might deploy: exactions or in-lieu fees, impact fees, linkage fees, special assessments, incentive zoning payments via contributions of infrastructure or cash, and transfer of development rights. These tools support municipal infrastructure, improvements, and programs, and help distribute the burdens and benefits of development more equitably within the city.

As new subway lines, roads, and other public works raise the value of nearby land and real estate . . . developers and property owners share that publicly generated windfall to help local governments pay for new bridges, transit, parks, affordable housing, and other infrastructure upgrades.

Land value capture is driven by concerns for efficiency and fairness. First, public investment in municipal improvements should generally benefit the public, rather than individual landowners. And developers should bear the costs of private development, not the community. Without this constraint, developers would have little or no incentive to curb consumption of public goods such as roads or access to sewerage services,

yielding inefficient land usage. Second, government actions that increase land values, such as regulatory changes to increase allowable densities on a lot, should also benefit the public. If, for example, a developer asks to construct a taller building than would normally be allowed, the city could require the developer to build affordable housing units or public green space in exchange. LVC requires that owners return the value generated by those modifications to the government that created them, so that it can then provide the community with additional infrastructure and services. As long as the regulatory changes are thoughtful and well planned, they can benefit all parties.

This report considers two contexts in which a municipality might recover increases in the value of land—also called "land value increments"—from property owners or developers. First, the city might seek payment from a property owner who passively receives a boost in land value resulting from an improvement initiated by the municipality, such as a subway line extension that dramatically increases the values of nearby properties. Second, the city might seek payment from a developer whose activities consume public resources and trigger land value increases, such as building to greater density. Classic examples of developer land value capture tools include exactions, impact and linkage fees, and special assessments.

Despite its sound principles and effective historical uses, LVC has been sharply debated among policy makers, citizens, and theorists in the United States. Discussions have sometimes drawn harsh lines between those resisting perceived intrusions into individual property rights and those seeking public benefit from public investment and other government actions.

This report considers those controversies, but the most important takeaway is that land value capture has in various forms been used and legally upheld in the United States for some 150 years. It remains a valid and viable option to finance government activities, provided policy makers leverage available tools appropriately. State and local law must authorize any land value capture tool that a municipality seeks to implement, and other complexities and differences exist across jurisdictions. Moreover, the Takings Clause of the Fifth Amendment to the U.S. Constitution places some constraints on land value capture: Regulations regarding LVC cannot "go too far," in the words of the Supreme Court, to limit the usefulness of an owner's property *(Pennsylvania Coal Co. v. Mahon*, 260 U.S. 393 [1922]). Exactions and fee requirements, for instance, must have an "essential nexus" and "rough proportion-ality" to the social costs of the developer's proposed project, discussed in detail in chapter 3.

Within these general guidelines, land value capture is permitted and can be expanded to produce necessary municipal infrastructure and other public goods, such as affordable housing or parks.

This report makes several recommendations:

- require developers to share the cost of infrastructure;
- capture value created by government planning initiatives and investment;
- reform the legal rules;
- recognize and plan for constitutional uncertainties; and
- build consensus, defuse the rhetoric.

The 1922 U.S. Supreme Court case *Pennsylvania Coal Co. v. Mahon* determined that land value capture regulations cannot "go too far" in limiting owners' use of their private property, after H.J. Mahon sued to prevent mining under his home out of concern that it would affect the land's integrity, as it had in Scranton and elsewhere in Pennsylvania. *Source: Courtesy,* Times-Tribune, *Scranton, PA*

CHAPTER 1

The Municipal Need for Land Value Capture

Municipalities face growing populations, increasing demand for new and refreshed infrastructure and services, and diminished federal and state support. Land value capture (LVC) presents an attractive revenue source, especially when it is framed as private landowners' returning to the community a fair share of wealth created by public actions or investments. LVC tools can use the market to draw upon additional sources of government funding and thus support municipal infrastructure developments, improvements, and programs—while more equitably distributing the burdens and benefits of development (Calavita 2015).

A 2022 bridge collapse in Pittsburgh, Pennsylvania, demonstrates why local governments need to find new revenue sources for infrastructure investment in the face of diminished state and federal support. *Source: National Transportation Safety Board/Wikimedia Commons*

Chapter 2 considers the American legal framework for land value capture in more depth. Notably, LVC has financed municipal government activities in the United States since the Civil War. The Fifth Amendment to the U.S. Constitution includes the Takings Clause, which the Supreme Court has interpreted to mean LVC cannot "go too far" in impinging on private property ownership. Within general guidelines and reasonable exercise, however, LVC is permitted to produce municipal infrastructure and programs, and is expandable in all 50 states.

High-speed rail construction, including in Fresno, California, is increasingly possible thanks to land value capture applications focused on transit-oriented development. *Source: Ryan Christopher Jones/The New York Times/Redux*

Increased Demand for Infrastructure Funding

A 2021 American Society of Civil Engineers report estimated that the United States infrastructure deficit is $2.59 trillion (American Society of Civil Engineers 2021). The Infrastructure Investment and Jobs Act, signed into law by President Biden in November 2021, authorized $500 billion above funding Congress had planned to authorize over the next eight years, but infrastructure needs still exist (Sprunt 2021). From 2007 to 2017, public spending on infrastructure fell by $9 billion in real terms, and real spending on capital projects fell 16 percent even as demand for infrastructure increased (Kane and Tomer 2019).

Urbanization has escalated in the United States over the past 50 years, and a dense, urban population

simply requires more amenities. Moreover, with growth in real income, the public has come to expect more of infrastructure, and demands for it have increased, resulting in calls for more sophisticated schools, athletic facilities, parks, advanced fire and police facilities, and social and cultural centers. New regulatory requirements like federal environmental mandates also obligate local governments to invest substantially in infrastructure such as water treatment plants.

Indeed, that additional funding has to come from somewhere. In 2016, transfers from the federal government comprised 23 percent of combined state and local general revenues (Urban Institute). While this figure has fluctuated somewhat over the past 30 years—with a dip in 1989 and a boost with stimulus funds post-2008—the federal contribution has generally remained at that 23 percent level. Thus, federal support has not grown steadily. Local governments, however, have rapidly increased infrastructure spending to meet public demand and needs as well as federal mandates. Direct general expenditures for state and local governments increased 190 percent from 1977 to 2019, rising from $1.2 trillion (in inflation-adjusted 2019 dollars) to $3.3 trillion in 2019 (Rocca, Duvall, and Palter, 2017; Urban Institute).

The Property Tax Question

The property tax is a key part of municipal finance, providing 31.8 percent of total state and local tax collections in the United States in fiscal year 2017 and 72 percent of total local tax collections (U.S. Census Bureau 2017a). The current U.S. property tax system offers an essential vehicle for land value capture: Municipal improvements raise the value of benefited buildings and land, and then that enhanced value is taxed. Under this system, developing a new park or public transportation hub should increase the values of nearby homes and commercial properties, and the reassessment of these properties should reflect that. If the tax rate remains constant, the

benefited property owners will pay increased taxes. The advantage of using the property tax system to capture the increased private value of public investment is that the government does not have to enact new legislation or create a new apparatus or administration to garner that revenue—if the area already has a property tax in place.

Even as infrastructure demand and obligations have increased, however, local taxpayers have organized to limit mounting property tax increases from inflationary growth in housing values. California's 1978 Proposition 13 was the first such "taxpayer revolt," wherein voters passed a ballot initiative to cap

Property Tax and Tax Increment Finance (TIF)

Property taxes can be an important form of LVC, as well-functioning property tax systems base obligations on the market value of real estate. But that link is not automatic. Rather, it depends on the enabling and administrative frameworks in place for the property tax. Land value increases in jurisdictions with well-functioning property tax systems should generate higher assessed values for properties near planned public investments—and such taxation does return some value to the public from private entities for the public sector. However, limits on value assessments or increases can restrict the property tax's success.

Many communities use TIF to promote economic development and community investment by earmarking property tax revenues from anticipated increases in assessed values within a designated district. Because TIF directs the use of existing property taxes, some observers may erroneously believe that it is a land value capture tool. More accurately, it is a way to transfer value from one area to another—rather than returning *additional* value to the public sector.

California's 1978 passage of the still-controversial Proposition 13 has limited local governments' ability to raise property taxes that fund schools, infrastructure, and other essential services. *Source:* Los Angeles Times

property tax increases. Amid this popular resistance, local governments still faced conflicting demands for increased facilities and amenities, especially infrastructure, as well as public services, particularly for centers with large or growing populations. In this context, various alternative revenue sources—such as impact fees, exactions, sale of development rights, and others—have become increasingly attractive to local governments.

However, a local government might choose to employ additional land value capture tools beyond the property tax for several reasons:

- The property tax system may not work as efficiently and effectively as it could to capture additional value created by improvements. Assessors must conduct new valuations constantly to reflect ongoing public improvements, and those new assessments must accurately reflect new values; the tax rate must also remain level, and enough revenue must be collected to pay for the public improvement. A delay is also likely before property values reflect the benefits of the improvements.

- Legislation may prevent the property tax system from being an effective vector for additional value capture. For example, limits on the

property tax rate to protect homeowners may also reduce the property tax system's efficacy in capturing land value increases.

- Some would argue that LVC charges for benefited properties should be distinct from the property tax and instead become analogous to a fund for initial capital investments. The property tax could then be used for ongoing operational municipal expenses.

- Political pushback, systemic inconsistencies, and other issues may present problems.

The property tax nonetheless remains an effective and stable means to finance public improvements and to capture for the public at least some of the property value increases that arise from public infrastructure investments. The property tax should thus be essential in municipal discussions of land value capture tools, even if it cannot operate alone in this regard.

Defining Land Value Capture

The value of land can increase due to demographic and economic factors that heighten demand, such as population growth, new employment opportunities, or a general increase in wealth and consumption

(Chapman 2017). The value of privately owned land, however, can also grow as a direct result of two types of explicit governmental action (Smolka 2013). First, public investment in neighboring infrastructure, such as a light rail station, can enhance the value of nearby land (Walters 2013). Second, land value might also increase if the government modifies land use regulations, such as a rezoning to increase permissible densities (Chapman 2017). Both of these government actions—infrastructure investment and expanded development rights—generate wealth by boosting land value (Kim 2020b).

The value of land can increase due to demographic and economic factors that heighten demand, such as population growth, new employment opportunities, or a general increase in wealth and consumption.

LVC is based on the "notion that the public is entitled to all, or a portion of, land value increases that result from public investment in land improvements or public actions that increase land value. . . . This recompense is predicated on a basic principle: those responsible for creating value should reap some, if not all, of the benefits" (McCarthy 2017, 2–3). In other words, without LVC, this increased land value remains exclusively in private hands despite the public actions that created it. In contrast, LVC utilizes various tools to capture (or "recover" or "return") this enhanced value for the public, enabling the recovery, to some extent, of the increases in private land value linked to government actions (Walters 2013).

As noted above, two types of public actions can increase land values and thus support land value capture. The first is public investment in infrastructure

and services, to improve local conditions or compensate for the impacts of increased consumption. In a common example, a municipal government builds a new light rail station on its existing system as part of a program to reduce automobile commuting or to encourage infill development. As a result, the properties near the new station increase substantially in value, because they now offer better access to jobs, amenities, and services in other parts of the city, and they may be more suitable for development, too. LVC principles dictate that these property owners owe the public all or a portion of their land's increased value by, for example, paying part of the cost to install the new station. These tools operate on the principle that individual landowners should repay the government for a special benefit or resource it has provided, such as a convenient new transit station. Reimbursing the municipality for extra improvements or increased consumption is fair, equitable, and economically sound. Requiring consumers of public goods to pay for them helps prevent overconsumption of those goods and ensures that producers of private goods pay associated costs.

The second type of action that enhances land value is modifying land use regulations to expand development rights. For example, a city's zoning ordinance could allow developers to construct buildings that exceed usual height limits to provide additional buildable space, accommodate housing or commercial growth, or conserve land elsewhere. In this scenario, LVC tools would ensure that the added value created by the extra height would return to the public, most often via new amenities such as a park, broader sidewalks, or even affordable housing units.

These cases can be more controversial. Many landowners believe that they always had the right to build and should be permitted to do so. In their view, when a government increases land value by modifying land use regulations, that action has simply restored the owners' inherent property rights, so the owners are not obligated to return anything to the government.

However, this perspective fails to account for the fact that an owner's right to develop the property is inherently limited. Individuals always relinquish some prerogatives in return for the benefits of a shared society with its norms and governance. In this perspective, the increased land value is still essentially created by the public and is thus a legitimate target for recovery. Deploying land value capture in this situation, however, does require a sensitivity to these competing visions and legal views.

Land Value Capture Tools

Once a government establishes how and when it has created additional land values that warrant using land value capture, it can choose from a range of tools. In practice, LVC includes a variety of mechanisms and policies, which jurisdictions implement differently across geographies and at different phases of a plan, project, or rezoning effort. Chapter 3 explores tools that recover increases due to public investments or special benefits given to landowners. Chapter 4 considers tools that recover increases due to changes in land use regulations to expand development rights. All these tools share one common goal: returning land value to the public.

LANDOWNER PAYS FOR SPECIAL BENEFITS

Exactions
Municipalities require developers to pay exactions to obtain approvals or permissions allowing them to build on a parcel. Exactions may take the form of land, cash, or other in-kind remunerations designed to defray the costs of new development—both the additional public services and the consumption of existing public resources required by a new project. In principle, a property's value will increase if and when an owner receives permission to intensify its use and impact on public services. Exactions then allow the city to recover the value of its investment

in public infrastructure from the developer. For example, a developer putting in a new residential subdivision may be required to dedicate land for a public park rather than compel the new residents to overcrowd an existing park.

LVC includes a variety of mechanisms and policies, which jurisdictions implement differently across geographies and at different phases of a plan, project, or rezoning effort.

Impact Fees
Impact fees are one-time charges that municipalities may assess against a developer to offset a project's capital, service, and social costs to the public—such as increased demand for water. An impact fee is usually considered a charge to offset a direct negative externality. Developers pay the municipality a one-time cash charge to cover the costs associated with a development's impact on certain public services and infrastructure, and the municipality invests this revenue in public services and infrastructure. For example, these costs might fund off-site infrastructure such as a school annex or enlarged sewage treatment facility, additional personnel for fire and emergency services, or affordable housing that otherwise might be lost because of the project. Impact fees usually differ from exactions in that they recover costs for off-site rather than on-site facilities, include capital construction for major infrastructure (such as a school addition) in addition to land dedication (when the developer deeds land in the project area to the city, perhaps to be used for roads), pay for public services as well as physical improvements, and apply to all sorts of developments, not just residential subdivisions.

Linkage Fees

Linkage fees differ slightly from impact fees, though they are similar. A linkage fee typically mitigates an indirect problem created by development, whereas impact fees are more direct. For example, linkage fees may be imposed on a nonresidential development, like an office or industrial building, to finance affordable housing elsewhere. The rationale is that the commercial development will increase demand and prices for local housing, necessitating more affordable options. Like impact fees, however, linkage fees still require developers or property owners to pay their fair share of infrastructure and service development based on the request for special permits.

Special Assessments

Local governments may impose special assessments on properties in a circumscribed geographical area to pay for specific improvements that benefit a limited number of properties. Examples include local sewer and water lines, street paving, neighborhood transit stations, and small parks. A local legislature can impose a special assessment directly, or a municipality can create a special assessment district to administer the program or facility, such as a small local park or street authority. Special assessment districts are also known as "local improvement districts" or "benefit assessment districts," depending on the state. Through a special assessment, the municipality recoups what it spent on increasing the value of the benefited properties without imposing on unaffected property owners.

LANDOWNER OR DEVELOPER PAYS FOR LAND VALUE INCREASES LINKED TO REGULATORY CHANGES

Governments can also recover all or part of land value increases resulting from zoning or other land use regulations. Altering permitted land use from rural to urban, for instance, or increasing the Floor Area Ratio

Figure 1.1
Floor Area Ratio (FAR) Illustrated

Every zoning district has a floor area ratio (FAR), which defines the permitted size of a building relative to the lot on which it is situated.

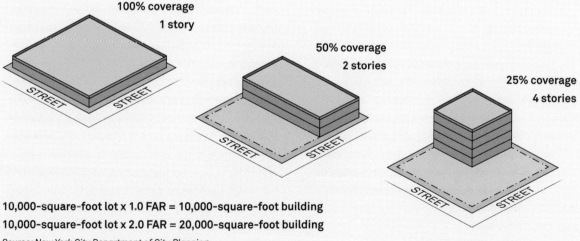

100% coverage
1 story

50% coverage
2 stories

25% coverage
4 stories

10,000-square-foot lot x 1.0 FAR = 10,000-square-foot building
10,000-square-foot lot x 2.0 FAR = 20,000-square-foot building

Source: New York City Department of City Planning

(FAR, or the relationship between a building's total usable floor space and the total area of the lot on which it stands; see figure 1.1, page 13) can generate value uplifts that government may claim.

In the United States, upzoning is a common regulatory change that occurs when a neighborhood is rezoned to permit more intensive development, thus increasing the value of landowners' properties.

In the United States, upzoning is a common regulatory change that occurs when a neighborhood is rezoned to permit more intensive development, thus increasing the value of landowners' properties. The municipality will likely presume that increased land value will also create incentives for developers to address important public policy goals. For example, allowing some multiunit housing in single-family zones could lead to construction of more affordable housing. Some upzonings even require the owner to provide certain community benefits (like affordable housing) to exercise the upzoning option. This allows the owner's land to increase in value and the city to recover that land value increment it created in the form of needed affordable housing.

The following tools are generally used to recover land value increases linked to changes in land use regulations. Some are deployed as "incentives," or opportunities that a government offers to private property owners or developers. Typically, owners or developers can exceed an allowed zoning regulation in exchange for creating new public assets, such as infrastructure or affordable housing units, that the city or market could not fund otherwise.

Incentive Zoning: Infrastructure

Incentive zoning laws allow a landowner to exceed statutory limits on building size, height, placement, density, or bulk if the owner provides certain public improvements, amenities, or services on the property or in its immediate vicinity. An owner may also access altered setback rules or similarly adjusted restrictions. Authorized owner improvements might include a public plaza or park, nearby transit upgrades, cultural or social programs, or affordable housing units. The landowner thus gains additional building rights, and the municipality captures a portion of the land's increased value in the form of the public improvements.

Incentive Zoning: Cash Contributions

Property owners and developers may also be able to receive incentive zoning benefits by making cash payments to the municipality rather than contributing public improvements. In this way, cities can recover at least some of the increased value associated with enhanced FAR while also directing that returned value to high-priority policy goals. Cash contributions may also go through a public fund to finance public improvements or programs in designated areas beyond the immediate neighborhood of the owner's property, allowing for broader spatial returns.

Transferable Development Rights

Zoning and other land use regulations limit the development rights for parcels. Some municipalities have legislation that allows an owner to sell and transfer unused development rights (TDRs) from one parcel to another. The receiving parcel owner can then exceed usual building limitations, increasing the value of that land. This TDR legislation, however, typically requires that the parties share a portion of the extra development rights with the municipality, by paying the city a fee for the transfer transaction. The fee generates revenue for subsequent public investments, and the transfer of density can also advance other urban planning objectives.

CHAPTER 2
The Case for Land Value Capture

During the Gilded Age, scholar Henry George inspired modern land value capture theory when he posited that the value of raw land increases not because of the owner's efforts, but because of general activities by the government and exogenous changes within the community. He believed, therefore, that the entire community—not only the individual landowner— was entitled to share in those increases (Fainstein 2012). George thus advocated for a high tax on raw land values and no tax on improvements made by the owner, rewarding owner initiative and capturing land appreciation for the public.

The under-construction Lechmere Square transit station in Cambridge, Massachusetts, seen in September 2021, has been funded in part by developers of the North Point site, seen at left. *Source: Phil/Creative Commons*

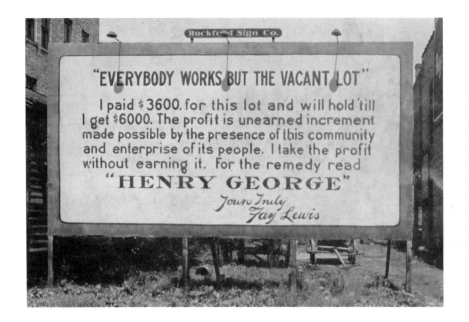

Rockfd Sign Co.

"EVERYBODY WORKS BUT THE VACANT LOT"

I paid $3600. for this lot and will hold 'till
I get $6000. The profit is unearned increment
made possible by the presence of this community
and enterprise of its people. I take the profit
without earning it. For the remedy read

"HENRY GEORGE"

Yours Truly
Fay Lewis

Scholar Henry George's work in the nineteenth century regarding capturing land appreciation for the public had widespread and lasting effects—including on Rockford, Illinois, landowner Fay Lewis, who erected this billboard in 1914—that continue to inform debates on land value capture. *Source: From The New York Public Library*

George underscored a key idea underlying land value capture: appreciation in the value of raw land that did not result from its owner's activities should be returned to the public. In George's system, the owner would contribute this portion of the increased property value specifically through a tax (Hagman and Misczynski 1978, xxxviii).

Some forms of land value capture go beyond reimbursement for public improvements (Calavita and Mallach 2009). Because owners are not responsible for much of the appreciation in the value of their land, the public has the right to at least some of the value that arises from governmental changes in land use regulation, as well as from infrastructure and other benefits (Alterman 2012; Smolka 2013). Actions such as upzoning are public policy decisions that create private value, which should therefore be returned to the public in some form, ideally as new infrastructure and public services (Calavita and Mallach 2009). Developers at times may counter this argument, claiming that higher property values reflect their own efforts to assemble land, obtain financing, and execute a vision (Chapman 2017). Despite these counterarguments, however, American law has long permitted land value capture, albeit with certain limits. While land value capture may seem new to the public debate and common lexicon, legal precedent has upheld it for more than 150 years.

Why Land Value Capture Makes Sense

Land value capture is robustly defensible in terms of public policy, economics, and equity. This is especially true of those tools that reimburse municipalities for public resources consumed by developers and for special benefits conferred to limited groups of property owners. Similarly, strong policy support exists for governments to recover the increased value of land due to changes in land use regulation.

LVC tools such as exactions, impact fees, and special assessments help allocate public resources efficiently and distribute benefits and burdens fairly across society. These tools can play out in several ways as a government recovers the cost of a specific benefit bestowed upon an individual property owner or small group of owners.

COST INTERNALIZATION AND EFFICIENCY

Land value capture helps efficiently allocate land resources by recovering costs from owners who have benefited from public investments and actions. Without a compulsory charge, holdout beneficiaries could and would simply refuse to pay. Moreover, if owners are not required to pay for infrastructure that they alone enjoy, as in the case of special assessments, it could distort the "market" for public goods. For example, benefited owners could become functionally subsidized by the rest of the municipality, absolving them of hard choices and leading to over-investment in unnecessary improvements. LVC in that case would prevent the undervaluing of public goods (Chapman 2017).

According to economists, efficiency demands that a free-market actor should not pass along the costs of its activities to the community and should instead internalize those costs. Exactions and impact fees clearly demonstrate how LVC can internalize costs: Local government requires developers to provide the infrastructure necessary to support their own projects (e.g., roads or water lines) and account for their work's impact on other more centralized infrastructure provided by the community. The costs of the public improvements should ultimately be capitalized into the value of the land. All things being equal, an acre of developable land with an impact fee attached to it will be worth less than an identical acre with no impact fee (Smolka 2013).

Development can also bring harmful spillover effects such as increased traffic, crowded schools, and burdened water and sewer service. Exactions and impact or linkage fees address this concern as well. Land value capture generally prevents developers from passing negative externalities of development on to the community.

COST RECOVERY AND FAIRNESS

Some policies support LVC especially where government has made infrastructure improvements that increase the value of specific properties, prioritizing cost recovery, cost internalization, and support for further public investment. In many situations, LVC tools like special assessments allow local government to recover costs of infrastructure improvements made to benefit a limited number of properties

Residents and local officials debate "Missing Middle" housing in Berkeley, California, at an April 2019 city council meeting. *Source: Kristen Tamsil/*Daily Californian

The Warm Springs BART Station in Fremont, California, generated enough land value increases in surrounding residential properties to cover the costs of its construction. *Source: City of Fremont*

(Alterman 2012). While public actions that benefit the general community should be funded by some general charge, such as a citywide property tax, the local government should be able to charge the costs of improvements only to those lots that benefit from them. Fairness demands that those receiving the improvement should pay for it; after all, the values of their lots will increase as a result. Parties receiving an advantage should not be able to shift the cost burden to others who do not benefit.

Various studies demonstrate how much public investment in infrastructure can increase the value of private property. One study, for example, showed that single-family homes near a new rail station in Fremont, California, increased in value between 8.97 percent and 14.85 percent between 2007 and 2018 (Shishir 2019). Between 2012 and 2016, the median sales price of office properties in transit-proximate areas in Boston, Hartford, Los Angeles, and Phoenix increased between 5 and 42 percent more than did those in areas farther from transit (APTA 2019, 8). An earlier study in Portland, Oregon, showed that proximity to light rail transit stations raised home prices 10.5 percent (Hong, Rufolo, and Dueker 1998). A 2011 analysis of some 40 studies concluded that pedestrian-friendly and transit-oriented developments increased the value of nearby properties (Bartholomew and Reid 2011).

General Concerns About Land Value Capture

Thoughtful legislation and administration can help resolve some practical issues associated with land value capture. Other issues present deeper, philosophical considerations.

PRACTICAL CONCERNS

LVC might pose a cash-flow problem for property owners. If a neighborhood has been designated for land value capture to reflect increased property values near a new rail station, owners of smaller properties may lack the cash or access to financing to pay an upfront charge like a special assessment. In this scenario, land value capture fees can force low- and moderate-income taxpayers to leave changing neighborhoods. Similar issues with rising property taxes have regularly prompted property tax relief mechanisms, with mixed results for local governments and owners.

Governments must take a nuanced approach to address the needs of owners unable to pay a high initial charge and to avoid displacing them, but this problem is not insurmountable. Some states, for example, permit deferral of special assessments for homestead property for persons older than 65 or members of the National Guard or Reserves who have beeen called into active duty (Minnesota Statutes). Some municipalities in the United States and in other countries allow property owners to pay LVC charges in installments over a number of years (Menomee Falls, Wisconsin, Code of Ordinanaces; Smolka 2013).

The administration of special assessments and other land value capture tools raises other questions that must be addressed. For example, how should a municipality determine which properties benefit from the public improvement and therefore owe a fee? Drawing those lines and assessing the benefits for those closer to and farther from the improvement site take political capital and legal wrangling, as well as research and collection. With careful study and attention, however, these barriers are surmountable. Given the public benefit, the costs are well worth it.

Thoughtful legislation and administration may help resolve some practical issues associated with land value capture. Other issues present deeper, philosophical considerations.

Although evidence shows that infrastructure improvements increase the value of nearby land—presenting opportunities to apply LVC tools—policy makers should be careful to estimate the exact value increase and thus the potential municipal revenue generated by imposing an LVC tool. Higgins and Kanaroglou (2016) reported on 60 studies assessing the effects of transit stations on property values. They noted significant differences between cities and even within a neighborhood in a single city. They found two reasons for these differences:

- the presence of good alternative transit options such as highways or bicycle routes; and
- varying factors beyond proximity to a hub, such as open space or pedestrian-friendly design.

Finally, it's difficult to gauge the total annual dollar amount of land value capture by governments across the United States, for at least two reasons. First, the value captured through some LVC tools is not easy to quantify. While impact fees and special assessments recoup exact dollar amounts, fixing an exact value on in-kind contributions is difficult. For example, the valuation of "privately owned public space" is complicated, given that it is still privately held, is open to the public only during certain hours, has terms of use, and is maintained at the expense of the private owner. Determining comparable amounts is difficult, and the cost of construction does not tell the whole story.

PHILOSOPHICAL CONCERNS

Critics of land value capture challenge the notion that the public has the right to recover increases in land value due to modified land use restrictions such as zoning. Hagman and Misczynski observed that "some may regard windfall recapture as unAmerican. Many Americans consider it right that increases in value that the public conferred . . . belong to the private owner" (Hagman and Misczynski 1978, xxx). This "property rights" perspective builds on the proposition that individual ownership rights are absolute and can be limited by government only under specific and narrow principles.

Rachelle Alterman (2011) observed that supporters of such unrestricted property rights believe that market forces yield a more efficient use of land than regulations and taxes do. These LVC critics also tend to blame the high cost of housing at least partially on excessive land use regulation. Furthermore, strict property rights proponents would likely argue that they should not be forced to relinquish their property's gains as a result of governmental improvements or regulatory changes (Alterman 2012).

> While understanding philosophical battle lines is important for policy makers, the essential task is finding and adhering to the required constitutional balance between the right to property under the Fifth Amendment and the power of government to regulate in the public interest.

The pro-land value capture position comes at the issue from the opposite direction and assumes that private property is necessarily subject to "social obligation" (Alterman 2012). American law reflects this view, recognizing that individual property rights are granted by government, as the public's representative. Thus, the individual's rights are subject to the limitations of land value capture, among other restrictions, such as the prohibition on nuisances or the right for airplanes to fly over. Under this "social obligation," owners would have to part with some of the land values that "dropped into their laps" as a result of government improvements or regulatory changes.

While understanding philosophical battle lines is important for policy makers as they build consensus and mitigate disputes, the essential task is finding and adhering to the required constitutional balance between the right to property under the Fifth Amendment and the power of government to regulate in the public interest. In *Murr v. Wisconsin*, 137 S. Ct. 1933 (2017), the Supreme Court of the United States summarized the tension between the individual's property rights and the community's need to alter them for the public good:

> A central dynamic of the Court's regulatory takings jurisprudence, then, is its flexibility. This has been and remains a means to reconcile two competing objectives central to regulatory takings doctrine. One is the individual's right to retain the interests and exercise the freedoms at the core of private property ownership. Property rights are necessary to preserve freedom, for property ownership empowers persons to shape and to plan their own destiny in a world where governments are always eager to do so for them.

> The other persisting interest is the government's well-established power to "adjust[t] rights for the public good." As Justice Holmes declared, "Government hardly could go on if to some extent values incident to property could not be diminished without paying for every such change in the general law" (*Murr v. Wisconsin* 2017).

The Constitution can, and has, accommodated land value capture. As long as municipalities respect certain principles, as discussed later in this chapter, they can lawfully utilize LVC.

Equity Considerations

As with most land use decisions, land value capture tools trigger considerations of social equity and equal treatment. In order to achieve the fairest, most effective policy results, these concerns must be evaluated, acknowledged, and incorporated into governmental decisions to apply LVC. Laura Wolf-Powers (2019) clarifies the fundamental challenge:

> [P]lanners need to look more critically at these [LVC] mechanisms' distributional effects. . . . The equitability framework in use by policy makers today is a narrow one: it endorses the public sector's recovery of the "unearned increment," but it is silent on the question of how to distribute it. . . . To whom will that economic value be likely to accrue after being recovered and distributed? . . . Who is involved in governing value recovery and allocation?

Factoring social equity into LVC decisions requires a deep understanding and reconciliation of larger local, national, and historical issues—in general and as part of broader land use issues. Concerns for social equity in land use regulation have increasingly been identified, but how they play out in LVC cases specifically merits ongoing study, refinement, and solutions (Fischel 2015; Whittemore 2017; Tagtachian et al. 2019). Meanwhile, policy makers might consider these key questions:

When the government increases the value of private land, who loses and who gains if an LVC tool is deployed? When governments choose not to impose value capture while developing infrastructure that will provide special benefit to some property owners, it amounts to an economic transfer from the government, funded by taxpayers. The regressive aspects may be particularly harsh if wealthier property owners benefit from transfers at the expense of their economically disadvantaged neighbors.

When value is captured by an LVC tool, where is it distributed? When government changes land use regulation and recovers some of the resulting increased value of private land, the choice of how and where to spend these funds will have implications for social equity. Selections might be unfair or inequitable if, for instance, the government "spends" its share of the value in the developer's neighborhood rather than an underserved area.

Who takes part in the decision-making process?
The process of capturing and distributing publicly created value should be transparent and inclusive from the outset. Historically underrepresented communities (in terms of race, socioeconomic background, geography, and other demographics) need a front-row seat at that table. Moreover, if property owners with political connections can manipulate decisions to their own benefit, confidence in LVC programs will be undermined.

What about the details? Each LVC tool may raise distinct questions about equity and fairness, as discussed throughout this report. For example, some have argued that exactions and impact fees might raise development costs too much to allow affordable housing. To achieve an efficient and equitable result, a broad array of stakeholders—elected officials, planners, developers, landowners, advocates, citizens, program beneficiaries, and more—should be involved in considering choices and courses of action.

Legal Considerations

Policy makers can deploy a land value capture tool only if it complies with local, state, and federal laws. Government officials, particularly municipal leaders, must ensure that their state authorizes the LVC tools at work and that the project complies with legal requirements.

Generally, state law governs the creation and operation of land value capture tools, subject to preemption by federal law. While tools are common across states, associated terminology and substantive requirements of state enabling acts and local legislation may differ. State legislation must authorize the use of an LVC tool by the state and its agencies or delegate this authority to local governments. Municipal governments must pass a local ordinance to operationalize and detail the planned land value capture program, in compliance with the state's enabling act. Additionally, judicial interpretations can differ across jurisdictions, as states have their own constitutions that may override local legislation. Each state's constitution is distinct and subject to the specific interpretation of the state's own highest court. Policy makers, therefore, must be aware of legal differences among states and among localities within a single state, ensuring with proper legal counsel that a proposal meets legislative, judicial, and state constitutional requirements.

Without considerations of equity and impact on existing residents, policy makers may end up displacing lower-income households—even inadvertently. *Source: Tim Trautman/Creative Commons*

The Takings Clause of the Fifth Amendment to the U.S. Constitution limits actions by the federal and state governments that diminish property rights of individual owners. The clause states, ". . . nor shall private property be taken for public use, without just compensation."

THE FIFTH AMENDMENT TO THE U.S. CONSTITUTION

The Takings Clause of the Fifth Amendment to the U.S. Constitution limits actions by the federal and state governments that diminish property rights of individual owners. The clause states, ". . . nor shall private property be taken for public use, without just compensation." A classic taking that would require just compensation occurs when government physically appropriates private land for road construction or other public purposes. LVC tools rarely involve physical appropriation, such as eminent domain, but three types of government land value capture strategies might present concerns related to the Takings Clause. The federal and state courts have been concerned with constitutional issues related to regulatory takings, the nexus and proportionalty of exactions, and upzonings that may favor one owner over another.

REGULATORY TAKINGS

A municipality might enact a regulation that does not involve the government physically invading private land, but from the owners' perspective it has the effect of depriving them of the essential use of the property. In such a situation, the owner might claim a "regulatory taking" of the property. That is, the government has effectively appropriated the land, akin to a physical occupation, because of the regulation. Such challenges have been brought against landmark regulations that prevent the alteration of historically or architecturally significant buildings and against environmental legislation. In those cases, the owners claimed that the regulation was so restrictive that the owners essentially lost all meaningful use of their property, just as if the government had physically occupied the land.

A regulatory taking claim might be brought against various land value capture arrangements if the challenger can argue that the government's regulatory scheme worked as a taking. The legal test, however, for determining whether a regulation is a valid exercise of policy power or a taking that requires compensation (or voiding) is by its nature ambiguous. U.S. Supreme Court Justice Oliver Wendell Holmes, Jr., stated in the oft-quoted test in the *Pennsylvania Coal Co. v. Mahon* decision:

> While property may be regulated to a certain extent, if regulation goes too far it will be recognized as a taking. . . . We are in danger of forgetting that a strong public desire to improve the public condition is not enough to warrant achieving the desire by a shorter cut than the constitutional way of paying for the change. . . . [T]his is a question of degree—and therefore cannot be disposed of by general propositions."

Federal and state courts have applied this fluid test in numerous cases over the years. It is hard to define firm guidelines for regulation; there is no precise number, or even a ballpark figure, for how much land value reduction federal and state courts will tolerate. The full circumstances and particular facts will determine the outcome. Good counsel can provide guidance.

American constitutional law would probably not uphold some more robust land value capture proposals that other countries entertain. For example, an ordinance to downzone a downtown's FAR from 10.0 to 1.0 for all properties and then require owners to purchase rights to build higher—as São Paulo, Brazil, did—would probably be deemed a regulatory taking in the United States (Smolka 2013). In light of the Constitution and American history, such limits on property rights and such a large transfer to the government could be found excessive. While that is inarguably ambiguous, it is nonetheless the standard that the law has imposed on governments and owners and the one that we have to navigate in the United States.

EXACTIONS: NEXUS AND PROPORTIONALITY

In a series of cases from the late 1980s, the Supreme Court found that Takings Clause violations could occur when administrative bodies or officials granted building rights or permits only if the applicant-owner dedicated a land interest to the municipality. Thus, in two leading cases, *Nollan v. California Coastal Commission*, 483 U.S. 825 (1987), discussed in chapter 3 with more detail, and *Dolan v. City of Tigard*, 512 U.S. 374 (1994), the court found that the land right exacted by the municipality had to bear a "nexus"—that is, a direct causal connection between the government's exaction and the proposed development's social cost—and "rough proportionality" between the size of the exaction and the social cost. The government cannot use the approval as an excuse to extract a generally desirable fee or easement interest.

In a series of cases from the late 1980s, the Supreme Court found Takings Clause violations could occur when administrative bodies or officials granted building rights or permits only if the applicant-owner dedicated a land interest to the municipality.

In a later case, *Koontz v. St. Johns River Water Management District*, 570 U.S. 595 (2013), the Supreme Court applied the same principles to the exaction of a monetary fee. Thus, the Court found that the obligation to make a payment to purchase a conservation easement on another property has the same nexus and proportionality requirements as a land exaction.

However, the distinction between adjudicative and legislative impositions must be kept in mind. The Supreme Court has applied its exaction rules only to adjudicative decisions—that is, when an official or an administrative body imposes an exaction as part of the review of an owner's permit. The Court has not yet extended these rules to legislative exactions. Whether the Court, or lower federal or state courts, will do so in the coming years could have a significant impact on the validity of exactions, impact fees, and linkage fees. If confronted with a direct case on the issue, the Court may hold that legislatively imposed exactions of land or money, impact fees, and linkage fees should be upheld in deference by the judiciary to legislative decisions. (The precision of an exact dollar amount schedule set out in the statute might also help allay constitutional concerns about reasonableness, nexus, and proportionality of the fee).

Upzoning and Land Value Creation

"Upzoning" an area to allow for denser development presents a significant opportunity for land value capture. The municipality can create new value by granting property owners new building rights, and if market incentives work effectively, the upzoning will translate into returned value to fund improvements desired by the municipality. Alternatively, a city could make upzoning conditional on the owner's contribution of a desired benefit.

A local legislature institutes upzoning to address a community need. For example, the county council could increase permitted residential density for all properties within a certain distance of transit hubs to encourage residents to use public transportation

rather than cars. Upzoning a large area of land would thus satisfy a community need, as seen by the legislature, although some jurisdictions might also enact it for a single parcel in connection with a specific development project. In that case, the owner and municipality would negotiate the change, and it would usually include public improvements made by the landowner (Kim 2020b).

Upzoning generally makes the affected properties more "buildable," and hence more valuable, because landowners have more options for what they can do with the lot. In theory, the owners of upzoned properties near a transit hub will then build higher-density buildings, raise their cash flow, and further increase the value of their properties for public recovery. Municipalities that require a public benefit

The mixed-use development at 50 Pennsylvania Avenue in Brooklyn, New York, reserves units for low-income, formerly unhoused, and senior residents through the mandatory inclusionary housing program. *Source: Dattner Architects/ Pennrose*

contribution in order to use the upzoning are, in effect, conducting incentive zoning, and the LVC is directly attributable to the contributed benefit.

Moreover, some municipalities allow owners to utilize liberal upzoning guidelines only if they provide specific public benefits, such as affordable housing or infrastructure improvements (Calavita 2015). For example, New York City's Mandatory Inclusionary

Housing (MIH) program applies to upzoned districts that have increased the building size available for residential projects (Kober 2020). A developer seeking to build in the upzoned area under the revised guidelines must provide affordable housing based on three options the legislation provides. However, the percentage of floor area dedicated to affordable units varies, depending on what percentage of area median income the tenant earns, among other factors.

Zoning amendments or changes that upzone only a single parcel or a small group of lots might be challenged as unlawful "spot zoning," which the public generally views as a special favor the municipality grants to a particular owner. Municipalities must be aware that certain courses of action might create value but could incite an attack on spot zoning, which is impermissible in many jurisdictions anyway.

Legal challenges to upzoning, however, are not easily sustained. Neighboring owners may claim that the upzoning did not comply with the comprehensive plan or other statutory requirements. Or they may raise constitutional issues, arguing that their equal protection rights were denied because another owner received special treatment. Generally, though, these claims do not prevail, and the courts tend to sustain the rezoning if it was "reasonable"— that is, if the upzoning stemmed from a public need for the change. Though any challenged zoning would be assessed under Justice Holmes's "too far" standard, if the zoning gives the owner an adequate return, then it will likely be sustained.

Ultimately, the Fifth Amendment provides the essential guidelines to and limitation on government use of land value capture. Though the amendment is fundamental to the American legal system and its political, economic, and socal history, its rules are complicated and at times frustrating to policy makers. However, with careful thought and reliance on good legal counsel, governments can craft LVC tools that meet policy goals and comply with Fifth Amendment protections.

CASE STUDY: OREGON RESIDENTIAL UPZONING

In 2019, Oregon's state legislature enacted a statewide upzoning of certain single-family zoning districts, overriding local laws to permit the development of duplexes in cities with more than 10,000 residents (Bliss 2019; Oregon Revised Statutes § 197.758[3]). This indirect land value capture allowed developers to respond to market desires for multiple-family housing in certain areas and to profit from meeting this demand. The city does not get a direct financial share of the developers' profits, but it does receive an indirect value boost from production of multiple-family housing that will increase affordable housing options and help fulfill a municipal goal.

Oregon House Bill 2001 further provides that, in cities with more than 25,000 people, all "middle housing" types—defined as duplexes, triplexes, fourplexes, townhouses, and cottage clusters—are now permitted in areas previously zoned for single-family housing (Oregon Revised Statutes § 197.758[2]). Local governments retain power over the siting and design of middle housing, but they cannot "individually or cumulatively discourage the development of all middle housing types permitted in the area through unreasonable costs or delay" (Oregon Revised Statutes § 197.757[5]). Single-family housing is still of course permitted in these areas; the legislation simply prohibits the city from denying owners seeking to build middle housing types on their property (Oregon Revised Statutes § 197.758[6]). The statute further obligates the covered cities to adopt land use regulations that permit middle housing within a few years, depending on the size of the population (2019 Oregon Laws, chapter 63, § 3(1) [H.B. 2001]).

This legislation purports to address the state's shortage of affordable housing by providing additional "middle housing" choices, rejecting single-family zones, and removing local bans on smaller, less expensive housing options (Budds 2020; Oregon House Committee 2019). Additionally, denser use of formerly

Figure 2.1

Portland's Residential Infill Project

Re-legalizing "Middle Housing" Citywide

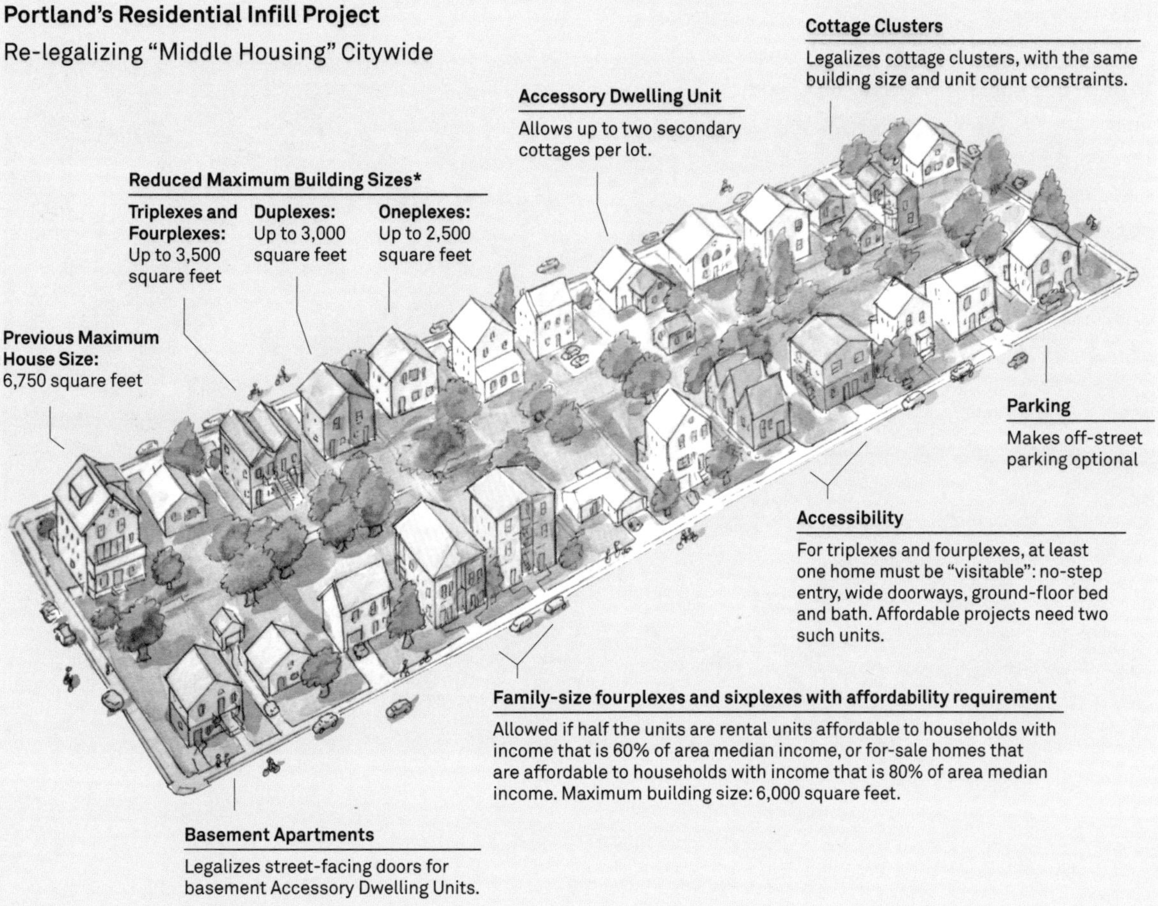

Cottage Clusters
Legalizes cottage clusters, with the same building size and unit count constraints.

Accessory Dwelling Unit
Allows up to two secondary cottages per lot.

Reduced Maximum Building Sizes*

Triplexes and Fourplexes: Up to 3,500 square feet

Duplexes: Up to 3,000 square feet

Oneplexes: Up to 2,500 square feet

Previous Maximum House Size: 6,750 square feet

Parking
Makes off-street parking optional

Accessibility
For triplexes and fourplexes, at least one home must be "visitable": no-step entry, wide doorways, ground-floor bed and bath. Affordable projects need two such units.

Family-size fourplexes and sixplexes with affordability requirement
Allowed if half the units are rental units affordable to households with income that is 60% of area median income, or for-sale homes that are affordable to households with income that is 80% of area median income. Maximum building size: 6,000 square feet.

Basement Apartments
Legalizes street-facing doors for basement Accessory Dwelling Units.

* Maximum building sizes based on floor area ratio allowed on a typical 50' x 100' lot in the R-5 zone.

Source: Illustration by Alfred Twu for Sightline Institute, sightline.org

single-family parcels helps reduce sprawl and commuting distances, and it can reduce the state's carbon footprint.

Oregon's preemption statute relies on market forces to motivate owners to sell their land to developers who will then build this housing, using that market response to increase value—meeting a municipal priority— in which the public shares. Markets are now free to provide more such desirable housing, as illustrated in figure 2.1, without the strictures of single-family zoning that drive up prices and suppress supply. In theory, individual owners also benefit from this action, because their land is more valuable when it can be developed for more intensive use. Governments can complement upzoning with land value capture policies to achieve goals that might not be achieved with the upzoning alone—creating more green space to serve an influx of new residents, or housing that is affordable to residents with very low incomes, for example.

CHAPTER 3

Land Value Capture Tools: Cost Recovery

The landmark 2013 Supreme Court case *Koontz v. St. Johns River Water Management District* concerned the Tarpon River in Fort Lauderdale, Florida, and found that monetary exactions are subject to the same legal requirements as land exactions. *Source: LuizCent/ Creative Commons*

When a government's actions increase private property values, it has a range of mechanisms and policies to recover those increases. The choice of tools, however, will depend on the enabling legislation in each state and the technical capacity of local governments. While the available tools vary, they share one common goal: returning land value to the public.

Land value capture tools fall into two main categories: those that recover increases due to public investments or special benefits, and those that recover increases due to changes in land use regulations. Each tool warrants contextual and legal consideration. This chapter focuses on the first category; chapter 4 will delve into the second category.

Exactions

Exactions allow a city to capture its investment in public infrastructure from developers of new projects if those projects have a negative impact on existing public improvements and services. A new housing subdivision, for example, may place an additional burden on the area's roads, in effect consuming an existing public good. Moreover, in principle, a property's value will increase if and when an owner receives permission to intensify the use of that property, increasing the impact on public improvements and services.

Municipalities may require exactions from developers as part of the building approval process in order to recover costs and share in the enhanced value resulting from municipal improvements. Traditionally, exactions comprised contributions of land in the development to be used for roads, parks, or retention ponds. More recently, though, exactions have also been required in the form of cash, sometimes known as in-lieu fees. These land, cash, or other in-kind exactions defray the costs of providing the additional public services required by a new development.

An exaction may be specifically required by enabling legislation or imposed by a governmental body or individual official in exchange for granting approvals. The latter case, wherein the government imposes exactions as part of an approval process, is often called a "negotiated exaction." Negotiated exactions may not be as predictable as exactions set by legislature, which can lead to municipal overreach or to

a developer's free-riding on past investments by the municipality.

Exactions often involve situations where governmental discretionary approval is needed, such as for permits. For example, *Nollan* and *Dolan*—two groundbreaking exaction cases from the U.S. Supreme Court—involved building-permit exactions. Moreover, a government may allow or even require an owner to pay an in-lieu fee and use the funds to purchase land or build infrastructure elsewhere, as in the other leading Supreme Court case, *Koontz*, which involved a monetary exaction wherein a developer had to pay a fee in lieu of dedicating an easement.

Exactions allow a city to capture its investment in public infrastructure from developers of new projects if they have a negative impact on existing public improvements and services.

Exactions serve land value capture goals by promoting efficiency and fairness, because those who benefit bear the cost. They promote efficiency by allocating the costs of development infrastructure to the development itself; any on-site infrastructure remains with the developer, who can pass its cost on to new owners. The municipality is not saddled with a cost that serves the new owners, who must pay their own way. If the rest of the community were forced to absorb the costs of the new development, it would create an economic distortion. But exactions also foster equity, because those who benefit from the improvement must pay for it, so the cost doesn't burden others in the community.

CASE STUDY: *NOLLAN V. CALIFORNIA COASTAL COMMISSION*

As the Supreme Court's first exactions takings case, decided in 1987, *Nollan v. California Coastal Commission* illustrates the increased scrutiny of exactions.

The Nollan family sought a permit from the California Coastal Commission to replace a bungalow on their beachfront lot with a larger home similar to others in the area. The Commission agreed to grant the permit if the Nollans granted an easement allowing the public to cross their property to reach the public beach. The Commission claimed that the new home would create a "psychological barrier" and obscure the view to the beach, preventing the public from recognizing that they had a right to access it.

In a 5–4 decision, the Supreme Court rejected the Commission's exaction requirement, which it considered to be an uncompensated taking. The Court stated that a local government's requiring excessive preconditions from a developer for issuing a building permit could be challenged as a taking.

The Court held that, to avoid a taking, the Commission must establish an "essential nexus" between the desired easement and the problems created by the owners' development plan. The Court rejected the presence of such a nexus in this case, finding that the easement, without compensation, did not address the concerns expressed by the Commission. It stated that "it is impossible to understand how [an easement to walk on the Nollans' property] reduces any obstacles to viewing the beach created by the house . . . and to understand how it lowers any 'psychological barrier' to use the public beaches" (*Nollan v. California Coastal Commission*).

The Court, therefore, rejected the validity of the exaction, finding a violation of the Takings Clause. The broader lesson of *Nollan* is that the courts will actively scrutinize the link between the proposed exaction and the reasons for it.

LVC OBSERVATION

Exactions and related in-lieu fees offer municipalities the opportunity to ensure that new developments absorb their own full costs, and to prevent free-riding consumption of municipal capital. Municipalities must deploy this LVC tool cautiously, however. First, exactions must be used within constitutional constraints, and administrators should prepare to face additional scrutiny in the future. Moreover, exactions essentially force payment for consuming municipal capital, and they are thus somewhat limited in their ability to generate new resources to realize public goals. While exactions—and, for that matter, impact and linkage fees—are designed to meet the demands of newcomers rather than existing citizens, they might end up providing certain economies of scale that benefit the whole town. Regardless, though, they prevent developers from consuming existing resources and are thus valuable LVC tools for municipalities.

Impact Fees

Impact fees are one-time charges a municipality assesses against a developer to offset capital costs, service costs, and social costs of their project. Developers pay the municipality a one-time cash charge to account for the impact their enterprise has on public services and infrastructure, and the municipality then invests this revenue in those amenities. For example, these charges might be levied for off-site infrastructure such as building a school annex or increasing capacity of a sewage treatment facility, for additional services such as fire and emergency personnel, or for preventing loss of affordable housing opportunities caused by construction of the project. The terminology often overlaps, but the term "impact fees" refers to charges that go beyond exactions to cover infrastructure, services, and off-site costs, rather than on-site land alone (Been 2005).

Local governments appear to be using a variety of impact fees more frequently to support a wider range of infrastructure types. Initially employed primarily to build sewer and water lines, roads, and parks, impact fees may now support fire and emergency services, transportation, police, storm drainage, watershed protection, affordable housing, and other resources. Impact fee legislation often sets out dollar amounts and formulas for specific fees to support specific improvements (e.g., roads and sewers) that may vary according to project type (e.g., residential versus commercial).

One-time charges to offset the costs developers impose for public services and infrastructure, impact fees may fund additional services such as fire and emergency personnel. *Source: kali9/ iStock/Getty Images Plus*

CASE STUDY: IMPACT FEES FOR SINGLE-FAMILY HOMES

A 2019 survey by Clancy Mullen of Duncan Associates reported on impact fees in 34 states, detailed in table 3.1, and found the national average impact fee for single-family homes that year was $13,627 (Mullen 2019b). This represents significant growth; in 2003, the average nonutility impact fee (which excludes water, sewer, and drain charges) for a single-family detached unit was $3,801, which had increased to $10,059 by 2019—a rise of 165 percent, shown in table 3.2 (Mullen 2019a). Even after adjusting for cumulative inflation of approximately 39 percent over that time period, the increase was still 90 percent.

LVC OBSERVATION

Impact fees align with land value capture principles by making a project's ultimate beneficiaries pay for the land development, promoting efficiency (Alterman 2012). The developer must internalize the true cost of the project, rather than pass it along to the community. Thus, the cost of new classrooms, for instance, is built into the development—either absorbed by the developer or paid by the home buyers.

Impact fees also promote fairness, in that those who create the expenses must pay for them. Developers and home buyers should not be able to compel the general community to pay the expenses of a new house, and impact fees prevent that from happening. Research on impact fees also shows that if developers (and, ultimately, their buyers) can purchase property without impact fees, the landowner (seller) will have to take a lower price from the developer. In that situation, "The cost of the impact fee is pushed backwards to sellers of the land . . . and sellers must reduce the sale price in such scenarios," which would also impede fairness (Evans-Cowley and Lahon 2003, 358).

Linkage Fees

While impact fees are usually regarded as a charge to offset a direct negative externality caused by a development, such as increased use of water, linkage fees typically mitigate more indirect impacts. For example, linkage fees may be imposed on a nonresidential development (such as an office or industrial building) to finance affordable housing, on the theory that the nonresidential development will increase demand and prices for local housing. In both cases, developers or property owners must pay their fair share for infrastructure and service development based on the request for special permits. However, the linkage fees address less closely connected negative effects.

> While impact fees are usually regarded as a charge to offset a direct negative externality caused by a development, such as increased use of water, linkage fees typically mitigate more indirect impacts.

Like impact fees and monetary exactions, linkage fees assess and recover the true cost of developing a new project. But linkage fees are distinct in that they are most often imposed only on commercial and office developers, typically in downtown areas. The rationale is that added commercial space will attract new employees to town, thus creating shortages in housing and upward pressure on rents in residential neighborhoods. Linkage fee regulations, therefore, typically require the developer to contribute to a fund that finances the construction of affordable units, often in areas not near the commercial development.

Linkage fee programs that require developers to provide affordable units within market-rate residential buildings also foster social and economic integration. The municipality could leverage linkage fees to build affordable units in neighborhoods where land and

Table 3.1

National Average Impact Fees by Facility Type in 2019

Facility Type	Single-Family Housing Unit	Multifamily Housing Unit	Retail (1,000 sf)	Office (1,000 sf)	Industrial (1,000 sf)
Roads	$3,691	$2,493	$5,970	$3,772	$2,143
Water	$4,249	$1,680	$654	$854	$889
Wastewater	$3,896	$1,986	$852	$1,217	$1,662
Drainage	$1,622	$852	$1,011	$815	$962
Parks	$2,993	$2,283	*	*	*
Library	$455	$344	*	*	*
Fire	$484	$370	$523	$503	$359
Police	$395	$295	$404	$270	$173
General Government	$1,573	$1,197	$665	$649	$388
Schools	$5,395	$3,134	*	*	*
Total Nonutility	$9,887	$6,476	$6,439	$4,640	$2,877
Total	$13,627	$8,034	$6,760	$5,407	$3,942
Total Nonutility (excluding California)	$6,743	$4,537	$4,952	$2,041	$2,041
Total (excluding California)	$9,841	$5,864	$5,228	$4,178	$3,147

Source: Mullen 2019a

Note: Totals excluding California are provided to offer a more accurate view of other states' generally lower fees.

*Rarely charged, except for park fees in Arizona and school fees in California, but included in totals.

Table 3.2

Changes in Average Total Nonutility Impact Fees for a Single-Family Detached Unit

State	2003 Sample Size	2007–2019 Sample Size	2003 Average	2007 Average	2011 Average	2015 Average	2019 Average
Arizona	27	27	$2,862	$5,196	$6,501	$4,707	$4,070
California	6	37	$12,857	$18,672	$23,849	$22,795	$28,918
Colorado	13	17	$5,205	$5,524	$6,859	$6,917	$6,898
Florida	33	67	$4,243	$8,601	$7,862	$7,568	$9,511
Maryland	9	10	$5,143	$8,588	$11,248	$11,486	$12,333
Oregon	4	11	$5,434	$6,000	$9,102	$9,104	$13,019
Utah	3	8	$1,763	$4,364	$4,745	$4,555	$4,357
Washington State	8	15	$3,501	$5,403	$7,115	$7,300	$11,849
All other states	49	74	$2,304	$3,163	$2,991	$2,964	$3,293
National Average	152	266	$3,801	$7,540	$8,593	$8,237	$10,059

Source: Mullen 2019a

construction costs are already lower, thus allowing for a higher number of affordable units, but that might perpetuate historical segregation patterns. Thus, municipalities must strike an equitable balance among social concerns. Examples of these programs in practice are detailed in table 3.3.

Notably, Boston, Massachusetts, has a longstanding linkage fee program with particularly robust receipts. The details of this program are indicated in figure 3.1. (Note that, although the figure's creators refer to exactions, this is a linkage fee program consistent with this report's definitions.)

CASE STUDY: ARLINGTON COUNTY'S AFFORDABLE HOUSING ORDINANCES

In December 2005, Arlington County, Virginia, passed an Affordable Housing Ordinance creating linkage fees for both commercial developments and residential projects (Arlington County 2005). The law indicates a baseline amount, adjusted by the Consumer Price Index for housing in the metropolitan Washington–Baltimore area, which at the time of publication was $5.48 per square foot for all gross floor area above 1.0 FAR. Developers may also meet their affordable housing obligation by including such units in their projects or off-site.

In a cautionary tale for proponents of linkage fees and inclusionary housing in general, however, this policy was preceded by a 2004 affordable housing inclusionary ordinance that opponents successfully challenged in state court. The judge found that Arlington County lacked authority under state law to require a cash fee or affordable units in order to approve a subdivision plan (*Kansas-Lincoln, LC v. County Bd. of Arlington*, 2004). Subsequently, the Virginia General Assembly had to amend the enabling act, leading to the 2005 zoning ordinance.

Table 3.3

Illustrative 2020 Linkage Fees in Select U.S. Cities

City	Construction Triggering Linkage	Target	Contribution per square foot
Boston, Massachusetts (Zoning Code § 80B-7)	Commercial and institutional construction exceeding 100,000 square feet	Affordable housing program, jobs program	$10.81 ($9.03 to affordable housing program, $1.78 to jobs program)
Boulder, Colorado (Revised Code § 8-9-1)	Office, retail, restaurant, hospital, institutional, and warehousing construction of any size	Affordable housing program	Office $24.14; retail and restaurant $16.08; hospital $16.08; institutional $10.00; warehousing $10.00
Cambridge, Massachusetts (Zoning Code § 11.200)	Commercial construction exceeding 30,000 square feet	Affordable housing program	$17.10 (reflecting $12 plus CPI escalation)
Denver, Colorado (Revised Municipal Code § 27-150 to 27-165)	Multiunit dwellings and other residential construction; commercial sales, construction services, and repairs; civic, public, and institutional construction; and industrial, manufacturing, wholesale, and agricultural construction	Permanent housing and supportive services for at-risk residents, low- and moderate-income workforce rental housing, and moderate income for-sale housing	Multiunit dwellings $1.57; other residential $.63; commercial sales, services, repairs $1.78; civic, public, institutional $1.78; industrial, manufacturing, wholesale $.42; agricultural $.42
San Diego, California, Municipal Code § 98.0610	Office, retail, research and development, and hotel construction	Affordable housing fund	Office $2.2; retail $1.28; research and development $.80; hotel $1.28

Figure 3.1

Annual Receipts of Boston's Affordable Housing Linkage Program, FY 1997–2016

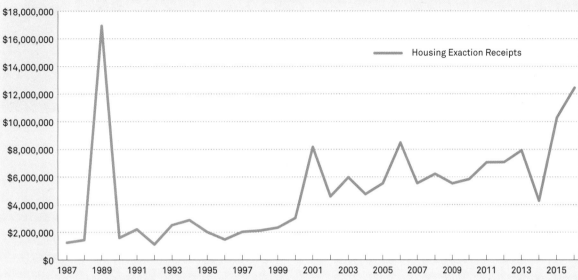

Source: Karl F. Seidman Consulting Services and ConsultEcon, Inc. 2016, Fig. 2

LVC OBSERVATION

Linkage fees reflect value capture considerations by preventing developers from externalizing local impacts. The developer must absorb the cost of depleting a municipality's housing resources rather than freely consume existing stock, which could negatively affect current residents. Linkage fees thus serve land value capture goals by making the developer—not the community—pay to provide housing for the commercial project.

Like exactions and impact fees, linkage fees help prevent developers from consuming municipal capital and shifting their costs to the city at large. If increased commercial construction will deplete housing resources in the town, developers should pay for their own consumption. Because linkage fees are, in a sense, reimbursing the community for resource consumption, they can't generate much additional value. But they

remain an important LVC tool to prevent developers from free-riding. Still, the courts may increase their scrutiny of linkage fees, based on constitutional principles elucidated in exactions cases, and closely monitor deference given to legislatively imposed fees.

Special Assessments and Special Assessment Districts

Special assessments are a long-recognized form of land value capture (Misczynski 2012). Imposed by local government on property in a circumscribed geographical area, they pay directly for special or local improvements that benefit a limited number of properties. For example, local sewer and water lines, street paving, transit stations, and small parks might be subject to a special assessment. Special

assessments can help a municipality recoup expenditures directly from the property owners who benefit. They may be imposed directly by the local legislature or indirectly by an administrative district created for that purpose. Special assessment districts are known by various names in different states, including "local improvement districts" or "benefit assessment districts."

By making landowners pay for infrastructure improvements that will benefit them specifically, special assessments connect expenses to outcomes and prevent property owners from free-riding by passing costs on to other residents who aren't benefiting. This is fair, for why should an owner have to pay for another owner's special advantage? It's also efficient, for why should government build infrastructure that beneficiaries are unwilling to pay for? Improved properties will presumably increase in value, offsetting the cost of the special assessment.

In 1980, a court in California justified special assessments in terms of fairness and efficiency:

> The rationale of special assessment is that the assessed property has received a special benefit over and above that received by the general public. The general public should not be required to pay for special benefits for the few, and the few specially benefited should not be subsidized by the general public (*Solvang Municipal Improvement District v. Board of Supervisors*, 112 Cal. App.3d 545, 552-553 [1980]).

Knox v. City of Orland, decided in 1992 by the Supreme Court of California, validated a special assessment for park maintenance. *Source: City of Orland Recreation Department*

Because special assessments pay for local improvements in a specific geographical area, they differ from a general tax all citizens pay for regular government costs. As the Supreme Court of California explained, a general tax is enacted "without reference to peculiar benefits to particular individuals or property. Nothing is more familiar in taxation than the imposition of a tax upon a class or upon individuals who enjoy no direct benefit from its expenditure" (*Knox v. City of Orland*, 4 Cal. 4th 132, 142 [1992]).

Special assessments helped finance much U.S. public infrastructure in the 19th century and into the early 20th century, but this trend hit a roadblock with the Great Depression:

> [D]evelopment projects closely tied to assessment bonds failed, landowners stopped paying assessments, and local officials . . . sometimes declined to force sales of property belonging to their voting neighbors to benefit distant bondholders (Misczynski 2012, 98).

In 1978, special assessments regained popularity in California after Proposition 13 reduced property tax revenues available to municipalities (Melnick 1993). Called "benefits assessments" in this case, they became another means to pay for essential government functions.

Special assessments are a useful land value capture tool, but some argue that "the amount of revenue generated in each instance is relatively small and limited in use to initial capital costs" because they can only be charged against specific locations (Iacono et al. 2009, iii). A 2010 U.S. Government Accountability Office report indicated that, of 55 transit agencies surveyed, special assessments financed transit projects only 17 times (GAO 2010). Municipalities could explore more opportunities to use special assessments for land value capture, as exemplified by the case studies described later in this chapter.

Special assessments can also support bond financing, as permitted by underlying legislation. When governments spread assessments over a number of years, cash becomes available to float

bonds so the municipality or developer doesn't need to expend cash up front (Froelich and Gallo 2014). By contrast, impact and linkage fees do not support bonds because they are one-shot payments, and future impact charges may not come to pass if development ceases.

Some municipalities create special assessment districts in order to impose special assessments. Terminology and procedures vary from state to state, and in numerous states, such as California, requirements differ depending on the type of service (for water, road, or sewer, for example). Sometimes local governments may establish a special district without direct public participation; other states might allow individual owners a right to be heard but do not require owners to approve special assessment districts (Maryland Local Government Code § 21-103; Michigan Statutes § 41.725). Additionally, some states allow a designated percentage of owners (for example, 50–60 percent) to reject a proposed district, as provided in Washington's Revised Code. Still others require approval by affected owners, as in Florida, where a majority must consent to business and historic districts (Florida Statutes § 170.01(3)).

In many states, a special assessment district remains active even after the improvement is built and paid for. The district continues to manage the improvement in question and to charge residents necessary ongoing fees for maintenance, replacements, and operations (Newport Partners and Virginia Polytechnic 2008). This is another advantage over impact fees and exactions (California State Legislature 2011). The fact that such districts can also be created and operated outside of traditional property tax regimes has made them a popular means of providing municipal services. As shown in figure 3.2, special districts have increased substantially in the United States over the last 80 years, including by 61.3 percent from 1972 to 2017 (or from 23,885 to 38,542) (U.S. Census Bureau 2017b). These districts might provide, for example, water, utilities, sewers, or roads.

Figure 3.2

Growth in Special District Governments, 1942–2017

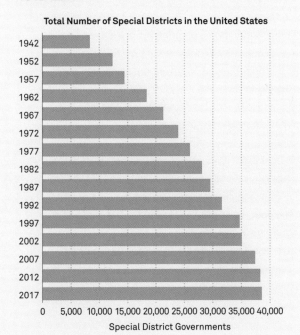

Total Number of Special Districts in the United States

Special District Governments

Source: U.S. Census Bureau 2017b

Businesses in Seattle, Washington, organized in 2005 to contribute to a special assessment that funded about half the costs of reopening an urban streetcar line that had been abandoned for nearly 65 years. *Source: SDOT/Creative Commons*

While state policies vary, many share legal requirements for a valid special assessment under statutes and case law:

- The improvement must confer a special benefit on a localized geographical area, rather than generally benefit the whole community. While some small spillover benefit is permitted, it must be comparably negligible. Thus, courts—including the Washington and Wisconsin Supreme Courts—have held that, for example, a public library cannot be built with a special assessment because it serves the entire community, but roads in a subdivision could be subject to a special assessment even though others in town might use them.

- The special assessment charged on a property cannot substantially exceed the special benefit received by that property; otherwise, the special assessment may constitute a taking. Moreover, this helps ensure rational alignment of costs and benefits by policy makers.

- When no statutory method is specified, the special assessment allotment among benefiting properties must be proportional, fair, and reasonable. Allocations may be based on the increase in property values, the distance of a parcel from the improvement (such as a small park or transit station), the amount of a property's frontage, the acreage of a parcel, or other methods.

CASE STUDY: SEATTLE SOUTH LAKE UNION STREETCAR

A special assessment funded approximately half the cost of reopening an urban streetcar line in Seattle, Washington. The existing 1.3-mile line, from downtown Seattle to the South Lake Union area, had been abandoned in 1941. The late Paul Allen, cofounder of Microsoft and then-CEO of Vulcan, led a group of businesses along Westlake Avenue to support reviving the streetcar line to help revitalize the area. In 2005, proponents petitioned the Seattle City Council to create a local improvement district that could help fund the new streetcar. Under Washington state law, owners of at least 50 percent of the area within the proposed district and 60 percent of the lineal frontage on the proposed improvement must sign such petitions. In this case, only 7 of the 750 owners in the proposed district filed formal objections, and the council approved the district.

The final estimated cost of the line before construction began was $53 million, and citizens in the local improvement district paid $25 million (47 percent of the cost) by special assessment. The land value capture here is evident, in that the city received a streetcar line at one-half the cost by requiring advantaged owners to pick up a large portion of the expense (Seattle 2005).

CASE STUDY: THE DULLES AIRPORT METRORAIL EXTENSION

Policy makers can fund infrastructure by combining several LVC tools to provide a revenue stream within their municipality to support a major project. When projects cross jurisdictional lines, localities can collaborate to approve LVC within each of their boundaries. A prime example of a recent—and major—use of special assessments in this way is the Dulles Metrorail expansion in northern Virginia, west of Washingon, DC. The Washington Metropolitan Area Transit Authority approved a 23-mile extension of Virginia's existing Metrorail system to Dulles Airport, Tysons Corner, Reston, and Herndon to alleviate roadway congestion now, and likely into the future, out of concern for the region's quality of life and economic competitiveness.

Pursuant to the Virginia Code, commercial owners petitioned to establish a special taxing district to raise funds for transportation improvements. Under the law, at least 51 percent of owners, as measured by either assessed value or land area, must approve a petition. In 2004, more than 64 percent of commercial owners in Tysons Corner approved Phase 1 of the project. Following public hearings, the new district was established with a charge of 22 cents per $100 of assessed value, in addition to the usual property taxes. Total assessments on Phase 1 were capped at $400 million, and the resulting five new stations and 12-mile extension of Metrorail's Silver Line opened to the public in July 2014. Commercial and industrial owners in Reston and Herndon approved Phase 2 of the rail corridor in December 2009, with a rate of 5 cents per $100 of assessed value gradually increasing to 20 cents and total assessments capped at $330 million. Phase 2 was scheduled to open for riders in 2020, but as of 2022, delays persist (Basch 2022).

LVC OBSERVATION

Special assessments provide policy makers an important LVC opportunity by allowing the government to improve specific areas without using general funds or taxing the entire community. Bond financing may be possible as well. Although property owners are statutorily required to pay, they must by law receive a commensurate benefit. Thus, municipalities have used special assessments to build freestanding improvements such as local street lighting, or improvements that are part of a system, like a train station. A government can generate significant new funding for civic improvements with a special assessment. Looking ahead, municipalities should consider expanding their use for LVC purposes, and state legislatures should eliminate legal hurdles to efficacy.

The Dulles Airport Metrorail extension project used a special taxing district to fund five new statiaons and 12 miles of new rail service. *Source: Timmons Group*

Mandatory Inclusionary Housing

Mandatory inclusionary housing reflects elements of linkage fees, impact fees, and exactions, and exemplifies a type of LVC that draws from various models. In some states, it may also be increasing as an obligation (Calavita and Mallach 2009).

The United States has a shortage of affordable housing, defined as housing that does not cost-burden its inhabitants by costing 30 percent or more of their income. In 2019, 48.4 percent of American households were cost-burdened, and an estimated 40.6 percent of renters spent 35 percent or more of household income on rent and utilities in 2018 (Mazur 2019; National Low Income Housing Coalition 2020). Inadequate affordable supply for the ongoing demand is viewed as the affordability crisis's key driver—exacerbated by an annual net loss of affordable units (Reina 2019).

In response, some jurisdictions have enacted legislation requiring residential developers to dedicate a certain percentage of units to moderate- or low-income residents to lease or purchase, if the project exceeds a certain size. In effect, the market-rate units thus subsidize the cost of building and, in the case of rental housing, operating the affordable units. Developers might absorb this cost themselves or pass some of it along to land sellers (Jacobus 2015). Prices on affordable unit resale are controlled to maintain affordability, and affordable rents are typically restricted for long durations—a minimum of 15 years, in some programs. Inclusionary housing mandates often grant developers subsidies or relaxed construction requirements, such as density bonuses, to offset the cost of building below-market units (Schuetz, Meltzer, and Been 2009).

Such legislation has been justified on various grounds: The community's economic and social health improves when people from mixed economic backgrounds live in the same building. Local employers will have enough employees at all wage levels if people don't have long commutes. In the past, exclusionary zoning prevented

Top: The city of Cambridge, Massachusetts, charges linkage fees on large commercial construction projects to fund affordable housing measures. *Source: Greig Cranna/Massachusetts Housing Partnership.* Bottom: Volunteers in Hawaii break ground on a new affordable housing project. *Source: Matthew Thayer/*Maui News

moderate- and low-income people, or families from certain racial or ethnic communities, from affording housing in the community. Housing supply is also inadequate for people lower on the income scale, seniors on fixed incomes, and minorities facing systemic, historical, and ongoing discrimination. Finally, when general housing supply is inadequate, high demand and high prices result.

By 2015, 866 jurisdictions in 25 states and the District of Columbia had at least one active inclusionary housing program, according to one study (Thaden and Stromberg 2017). Three states accounted for 89 percent of the total jurisdictions surveyed:

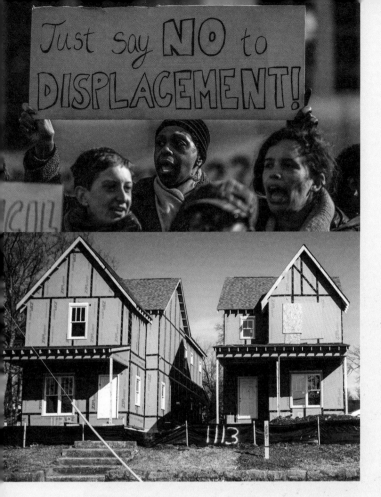

Top: New York City has applied land value capture tools to numerous high-profile housing projects, not without controversy. *Source: Erik McGregor.* Bottom: State legislation in Tennessee prohibits local mandatory inclusionary housing laws. *Source: Michael W. Bunch/Nashville Scene*

New Jersey (45 percent), Massachusetts (27 percent), and California (17 percent). These figures include both mandatory and voluntary on-site programs, as well as impact fees for off-site affordable housing. No clear data show that lower pricing for inclusionary housing units has reduced land sales and construction and diminished housing supply (Jacobus 2015).

State legislation in Arizona, Florida, Kansas, Tennessee, Texas, and Wisconsin prohibits local mandatory inclusionary housing laws (Arizona Revised Statutes Annotated § 9-461.16; Florida Statutes § 125.01055; Kansas Statutes Annotated § 12-16, 120; Tennessee Code § 66-35-102; Texas Local Government

Code, title 7, § 214.905; Wisconsin Statutes Annotated § 66.1015[3]). Courts in other states, such as Colorado, have also restricted mandatory inclusionary housing (*Town of Telluride v. Lot Thirty-Four Venture*, 3 P.3d 30; [Colorado Supreme Court 2000]). The Supreme Court of Virginia actually rejected mandatory inclusionary zoning outright in 1973 as being beyond the scope of zoning powers, calling it "socioeconomic" zoning (*Bd. of Supervisors v. De Groff Enterprises, Inc.*, 198 S.E.2d 600 [Va. 1973]). Other courts, however, have disagreed, most notably the New Jersey Supreme Court in its *Southern Burlington County NAACP v. Mt. Laurel II*, 456 A.2d 390 (N.J. 1983) decision.

In 2015, the California Supreme Court rejected a challenge to mandatory inclusionary zoning in *California Building Industry Association v. City of San Jose*, 351 P.3d 974 (2015). The builders' association questioned a city ordinance that required developers of projects with 20 or more units to sell 15 percent of them at an "affordable price." The court, however, discounted the argument that these conditions were an improper exaction and saw the ordinance as only "plac[ing] a limit on the way a developer may use its property." In effect, the decision characterized San Jose's ordinance as a police power regulation, not an exaction of a property interest. Moreover, this legislation did not rise to the level of a regulatory taking, under Justice Holmes's "too far" test, because it did not deny a fair and reasonable return to the developers.

Any benefits that a city provides a developer under a mandatory inclusionary housing program may help counter a takings argument, such as subsidies or construction concessions that compensate the developer and can mitigate loss of value resulting from the mandatory program. This scenario is similar to *Penn Central Transportation Company v. New York City,* 438 U.S. 104 (1978), discussed in chapter 4, wherein the transferable development rights available to the owner for landmarked property factored into the Supreme Court's finding that the owner had not suffered a compensable taking.

CHAPTER 4

Land Value Capture Tools: Regulatory Changes, Upzoning, and Incentives

Developers in the South Loop neighborhood of Chicago, Illinois, have increased their building rights by paying cash contributions enabled by incentive zoning policies. *Source: Mark Segal*

Governments can also recover land value that accrues to owners from changes in land use regulations. Zoning changes, such as permitting rural land to become urban or allowing more housing units on a lot, can generate land value uplifts that government may claim.

Upzoning—when local government changes neighborhood zoning to permit more intensive development—is common throughout the United States. The municipality typically seeks to incentivize private owners to address important public policy goals—such as creating more housing, increasing the number of businesses near a transit hub, or building up an area targeted for revitalization. Local governments can also require an owner or developer to actively (rather than incidentally) contribute to public policy goals by requiring fees or in-kind contributions in exchange for the right to develop more intensely.

The tools detailed in this chapter generally recover land value increases resulting from government actions, rather than from the government investments discussed in chapter 3. Whether deployed as incentives or requirements, however, each tool allows private property owners to exceed an allowed regulation in exchange for funding or creating necessary public assets the city would not otherwise have.

Incentive Zoning: Infrastructure

"Incentive zoning" ordinances grant a developer special benefits to provide a public good as part of a private building project. In this noteworthy use of land value capture, the city specifically receives infrastructure—rather than cash or other in-kind payments—in exchange for increasing the owner's development rights. Incentive zoning is an especially robust method of land value capture, as it allows the city to create new value to then capture via amenities or additional infrastructure investments that broadly benefit the public (Kim 2020b).

Most often, the incentive is increased density—that is, allowing a landowner to exceed statutory floor-area ratio (FAR) limitations for a building's size and location on a particular type of property. An owner may then be permitted to build taller structures, include more units or rooms, alter setback rules, and adjust similar restrictions—all enlarging a structure and increasing the property's value. In exchange, the owner provides certain public improvements, amenities, or services.

Incentive zoning is an especially robust method of land value capture, as it allows the city to create new value to then capture via amenities or additional infrastructure investments that broadly benefit the public.

Public goods sought in exchange for incentive zoning opportunities vary but could include open space, public space, affordable housing, street-level businesses, public transit improvements, and more. In a basic example, legislation might allow a builder to increase the FAR of a residential building in exchange for providing a street-level "pocket park," open to the public but owned by the landowner. The incentive could also offer developers expedited approvals and permits or waived construction requirements like off-street parking, rather than increased density.

Some 18.9 percent of U.S. local governments use incentive zoning (Homsy, Abrams, and Monastra 2015). In most places, the state must delegate power to enable local governments to pass incentive zoning ordinances (Maryland Land Use Code § 7-101–7-104). These acts typically use similarly broad language in two ways: first, to define the type of contributions that developers might make (namely, "amenities" or "a public benefit"), and, second, to describe the nature of benefits that the developer could receive from government ("other benefits") (Massachusetts General Laws ch. 40A, § 9). Once enacted, these regulations give local governments flexibility to meet current public needs and craft their own incentives accordingly.

Other statutes enabling incentive zoning are narrower, limiting developer incentives to building "bonuses" that require specific issues to be addressed, such as affordable housing (Connecticut Gen. Stat. Ann. § 8-2g), open space (Colorado Rev. Stat. Ann. § 30-28-401), or infill development to reduce sprawl (*Angstman v. City of Boise*, 917 P.2d 409 [Idaho App. 1996]).

Regardless, local governments must ultimately enact their own incentive zoning ordinances, as exemplified in table 4.1. These must fall within the power granted by the state, and the particular plan must be consistent with the enabling legislation (e.g., Maryland Land Use Code § 7-101[9]).

Incentive zoning gives the public direct, concrete benefits and spares the municipality even initial financial expenditures. Moreover, it injects flexibility into an otherwise rigid zoning matrix by allowing developers to increase their footprints and providing needed social improvements that government cannot afford. That said, incentive zoning is a voluntary system, so the payoff must be sufficient to motivate developers—meaning it will likely be effective only if demand for additional development prompts developers to capitalize on increased density (Calavita 2015).

Whether other incentives, such as expedited review or construction requirement waivers, would be enough remains to be seen. In the era of COVID-19, owners and cities might need to find new incentives that both sides find attractive if increased building sizes in central cities are no longer as attractive given increased commercial vacancies (David 2022).

Table 4.1

Illustrative Incentive Zoning Programs

Locality	Contribution	Incentive Bonus
Austin, Texas (Land Development Code § 25-1 and 25-2)	Affordable housing (10 percent of units must be affordable)	Increased height via FAR, waiver of off-street parking, minimum lot size, or fee concessions (depending on district)
Leland Township, Michigan (Zoning Ordinance § 17.01H.3.b)	Affordable housing and open space (10 percent of housing in a planned unit development must be affordable to persons earning 80 percent of area median income, and 55–60 percent of the development must be open space)	Up to 10 percent additional dwelling units for affordable housing contributions; 10–20 percent additional dwelling units for open space contributions
Middlesex County, Virginia (Zoning Ordinance § 15B-4)	Open space; residential, mixed-use community for persons 55 years and older	1 percent increase in density per additional 10 acres of open space; 5 percent increase in overall density for development of senior residential community
Downtown District, Providence, Rhode Island (Zoning Ordinance § 603)	Active ground-floor uses, including publicly accessible restaurants, retail, cultural, entertainment; publicly accessible open space; parking structures	Increased height of 10–30 percent for active ground-floor uses or open space; additional square footage to building per square foot of parking
Downtown District, Seattle, Washington (Municipal Code, § 23.49.012 and 23.49.013)	Affordable housing (rental for low-income households and 50-year dedication or sale to low-income households); childcare facilities (with 20 percent reserved for low-income households); open space; street-level human services offices, public restrooms, and transit stations	Increase in FAR (depending on building location, size, and contribution)

A carefully framed incentive zoning ordinance will likely withstand a takings challenge. If landowners receive only very limited building opportunities under the existing zoning ordinance and can obtain a meaningful FAR only by participating in an incentive program, they might prevail by claiming that the baseline regulation "goes too far" and prevents a reasonable use of the property. Under such a scheme, the only way for an owner to reach a "reasonable" level of development would be to "pay" for it by building infrastructure to access the "bonus"—not extra building rights but a "reasonable" use. Thus, this case involves a taking because the incentive system was used to extract property from the owner without compensation (*Montgomery County v. Woodward & Lothrop, Inc.*, 376 A.2d 483 ([Md. 1977]).

However, if the basic zoning regulation grants owners reasonable returns on their property and avoids a regulatory taking claim, then incentive zoning should not create a new takings problem. The owner may freely use the property without seeking an incentive and with constitutionally adequate returns. If the

A developer may create a privately owned public space (POPS) such as this plaza at 56th Street and Madison Avenue in New York City, in exchange for the right to build higher and denser. *Source: Jim Henderson/Creative Commons*

owner then voluntarily enters into what is essentially a contractual arrangement with the municipality for additional FAR, based on the owner's assessment that the exchange is fair and adequate, the law has no reason to intervene.

CASE STUDY: NEW YORK CITY

A 2015 survey indicated that 17.2 percent of New York State local governments used incentive zoning, with higher use in cities (20.5 percent) and towns (20.7 percent) than in villages (11.2 percent) or counties (9.8 percent) (Homsy, Abrams, and Monastra 2015). The state's enabling act allows cities, towns, and villages to adjust "permissible population density, area, height, open space, use, or other provisions of a zoning ordinance" in exchange for "open space, housing for persons of low or moderate income, parks, elder care, day care, or other specific physical, social, or cultural amenities, or cash in lieu thereof, of benefit to the residents of the community" (New York General City Law § 81-d[1][a], [b]). Local governments must enact specific zoning provisions consistent with these acts.

New York City's local ordinance, among other provisions, grants increased density to developers that provide subway station improvements and public plazas (New York City Zoning Law § 74-76, § 74-634). Developers have thus created plazas and pocket parks on private land and open for public use, known as privately owned public space (POPS). In exchange, the owner receives increased FAR, decreased setback requirements, or other concessions to increase buildable space. In short, developers can build higher and denser by allowing some public access. This has yielded 333 POPS locations in New York City—just one aspect of land value capture embedded in this incentive zoning program (New York City, Office of the Comptroller 2017).

> With strong data, standards, and effective management, the improvements created by incentive zoning can be truly appreciated by the public, especially those on property remaining under private ownership, like privately owned public space.

The city has faced two major operational problems with its POPS program, however. First, no complete listing of POPS existed until Jerold Kayden published an inventory in 2000, even though such spaces were first authorized nearly 40 years earlier, in 1961 (Kayden 2000). The Department of Buildings, the agency responsible for enforcing public rights in POPS, only began compiling its own database of these properties in 2015 (New York City, Office of the Comptroller 2017).

As a result, the public was unaware of many accessible areas, and governmental enforcement of that access was hindered. Moreover, a 2017 audit found that the Department of Buildings had not inspected 275 of the 333 POPS (83 percent) in the prior four years, and more than half of the inspected POPS were out of compliance with governing rules—about the same percentage of noncompliance as in the late 1990s (New York City, Office of the Comptroller 2017). Clearly, good recordkeeping and inspections are essential.

Second, design and operating rules for POPS under incentive zoning (including but not limited to open hours and user behavior) should be clear, with limits on owners' power to set essential rules. New York City upgraded its design and programmatic standards in 2007 and 2009, setting requirements for prescribed hours, making owners responsible for maintenance and sanitation, and encouraging POPS to follow the city's code of conduct for public parks (New York City Zoning Resolution § 37-70; New York City, Department of City Planning).

With strong data, standards, and effective management, the improvements created by incentive zoning can be truly appreciated by the public, especially those on property remaining under private ownership like POPS. Operational concerns do not undermine the essential benefits of incentive zoning and its utility as a value capture tool.

LVC OBSERVATION

Incentive zoning offers the municipality a tremendous opportunity for significant value capture—and for the city to control the process and the consideration that it receives. By granting increased development rights, construction options, or fee concessions to landowners, the city can use the zoning code to create new or enhanced property values. And by requiring owners to provide infrastructure, civic improvements, or services in exchange, the city captures part of that new value. Owners and the public both gain.

Incentive Zoning: Cash Contributions

The land value capture principle of exchanging zoning incentives for cash contributions is the same as for in-kind incentive zoning: A city grants a property owner increased building rights in exchange for a cash contribution for the associated increased property value. The legalities should be the same as with in-kind infrastructure improvements under incentive zoning, discussed above. This, however, is a notably potent land value capture tool, as the city creates new value and then recovers it via cash payment.

The City of Chicago's Downtown Zoning District uses developers' cash contributions from that area to stimulate commercial development elsewhere in the city. *Source: Mlenny/iStock/Getty Images Plus*

CASE STUDY: THE CHICAGO DOWNTOWN ZONING DISTRICT

The City of Chicago offers an especially noteworthy variation on incentive zoning. When owners receive the incentive, 90 percent of their cash contribution is not used in the Chicago Downtown Zoning District in which their developments are being built. Rather, the payment goes to a fund dedicated to stimulating commercial development in underserved areas. The Chicago plan is designed chiefly as a land value capture tool that broadly benefits the city, rather than one that mitigates neighborhood externalities caused by the new development. The developer contributes a portion of the benefit of increased building rights to a fund for general civic enhancement.

The 2016 Downtown Zoning District directed 80 percent of cash contributions to a Neighborhood Opportunity Fund that provides commercial

The owners of Grand Central Terminal in New York City transferred 666,766 square feet of development rights to JPMorgan Chase in 2018. *Source: Alex Proimos/Flickr*

development in underserved neighborhoods; 10 percent goes to a Landmark Fund to restore properties designated landmarks by city council. Thus, 90 percent of the contribution is for general civic enhancement, and the remaining 10 percent goes to a Local Impact Fund for public improvements within one mile of the development site. This contrasts with New York City's incentive zoning legislation, for example, which requires the improvements to be on or near the development property.

In Chicago, the City makes commitments when its council approves the zoning application and collects revenues when developers apply for a building permit

(City of Chicago 2018). By early 2020, the Neighborhood Opportunity Fund had $190 million in commitments and $68.2 million in collected funds, with approximately $35.5 million allocated to more than 100 projects (City of Chicago 2020). The largest payment to date, $18.3 million, was for the Bank of America Tower. For all three funds, the downtown Chicago bonus system totaled $237 million in commitments and $85.2 million in collections over the first four years (Spielman 2020).

LVC OBSERVATION

Like incentive zoning ordinances that require infrastructure improvements, a zoning program that increases FAR or other building requirements in exchange for a cash payment is a powerful form of land value capture. The city can cleanly create new value, recover the portion of the linked increase, and use the funds or return to pay for civic improvements throughout town.

Transferable Development Rights

Transferable Development Rights (TDRs) allow landowners to transfer the right to build from one property to another, under local zoning or other land use regulations. Effectively, the owner pays a governmental fee to transfer the unused density potential of one tract of land to a noncontiguous parcel of land better suited to greater densities. The fee in turn generates revenue for public investment.

For example, TDRs have been used in connection with landmarking laws, which typically prevent an owner from building to the usual FAR permitted by zoning if that will compromise an architectural feature of the landmarked structure. TDR laws often allow landmarked owners to sell their unused rights to nearby developers and thus recover some of their lost construction allowance.

TDR arrangements provide a significant LVC opportunity for cities to further urban planning objectives. The value of TDRs, for example, was a key factor in finding that the New York City Landmarks Law did not constitute an improper taking of the Penn Central Transportation Company's ownership interest in Grand Central Terminal *(Penn Central Transportation Company v. New York City)*.

New York City allows TDRs, provided the city receives a return from the sales price of the TDR, and new value is created by transferring the TDRs from the sending site to the receiving site, which expands the latter's ability to build. For owners, this increases the number of possible buyers, and with more potential buyers bidding, the price for the TDRs may increase as well.

The right, extent, and circumstances for the use of TDRs vary and depend on local zoning laws, as the examples in table 4.2 show.

Table 4.2

Illustrative Transferable Development Rights Legislation

Locality	Purpose	Description
King County, Washington (County Code §§ 21A.37.010 to 21A.37.16)	Limit sprawl and protect surrounding rural areas	Sending sites are rural areas, forests, and urban separator areas that undertake conservation easements. Receiving sites are primarily urban, with TDRs sold to developers. A county-sponsored TDR bank often acts as intermediary.
Mequon, Wisconsin (Zoning Ordinance § 58-332)	Protect nature preserve from bordering development	Sending sites are parcels that border a preserve and can assume conservation easements in exchange for TDRs. Receiving sites are then able to increase density.
Montgomery County, Maryland (Zoning Ordinance § 4.2.1)	Preserve agricultural and open space	The county downzoned 90,000 acres to agricultural land and allowed owners to send TDRs to designated receiving sites to increase residential density.
Portland, Oregon (Zoning Code § 33.564.070)	Provide housing opportunities and reduce pressure on environmentally sensitive areas	Sending sites are within Pleasant Valley Natural Resources Area. Receiving sites are specifically identified for residential construction only, with density not to exceed 150 percent of allowable development rights. (This is one of many Portland TDR programs.)
Warwick Township, Pennsylvania (Zoning Ordinance § 340-45)	Preserve agricultural land and develop senior housing	Sending sites are agricultural areas. Receiving sites are the designated Campus Industrial Zone and any senior housing project. The township often acts as an intermediary, purchasing and then reselling TDRs to potential developers.

With a $208 million purchase of transferable development rights from a nearby landmarked property, JPMorgan Chase was able to begin building a new global headquarters in Manhattan that exceeds the site's usual height and density limitations.
Source: Michael T. Young

JPMorgan Chase Global Headquarters: First Midtown East Project

In February 2018, six months after New York City passed the Midtown East rezoning, JPMorgan Chase announced plans to raze its existing headquarters at 270 Park Avenue and build a new 70-story, 2.5-million-square-foot headquarters at the same location. The project, based in the Midtown East district, was predicated on the use of TDRs from a landmarked property also within the 78-block area. Rumors about the sending site abounded until it emerged that the owners of Grand Central Terminal had sold JPMorgan Chase 666,766 square feet of TDRs for approximately $208 million. In May 2019, the New York City Council approved the new JPMorgan Chase headquarters as the first site to enjoy the Midtown East rezoning, and the company paid $42 million to the Public Realm Improvement Fund, reflecting the fund's share of the TDR sale.

TDRs can also be used as a direct value capture tool when municipalities like Los Angeles create them on condition that owners return part or all of the increased land value to the city through a cash or in-kind contribution (Los Angeles Zoning Code § 14.5.1–14.5.12). These laws should not pose any takings problem, as long as the baseline use granted to the owner provides an adequate return, as with incentive zoning.

CASE STUDY: MIDTOWN EAST IN NEW YORK CITY

In 2017, New York City amended local regulations so that a Midtown East zoning district of 78 blocks on Manhattan's East Side could revitalize this office district (New York City Zoning Resolution § 81-60–81-66). This rezoning would, ideally, allow the area to stay competitive with more modern and dense office structures, thus increasing employment. To incentivize owners to rebuild or expand their properties, the base FAR for commercial land was raised from 10 to 15. By granting additional property rights to owners, the city was able to recover some or all of the property value increases linked to those enhanced rights.

Owners of New York City landmarked buildings cannot alter the exterior of their buildings, but they can sell and transfer their otherwise unusable developable air rights over those buildings. Under general New York state law, however, owners of landmarked buildings could transfer these TDRs only to adjacent properties, limiting the value of both the rights and the landmarked properties because so few owners could bid to purchase the rights (Brenzel 2017).

The 2017 zoning amendment substantially expands the geographic transferability of TDRs in Midtown East, allowing owners of landmarked buildings to sell and transfer TDRs to any property within the Midtown East development district. This added significant value to the 33 landmarked properties in the area, the top four of which are included in table 4.3. The amendment also includes another land value capture component, which requires a seller to pay the city $61.49 per square foot of transferred air rights (or 20 percent, if the price is more than $307.45 per square foot) (Brenzel 2017).

Funds captured through this program are placed in a Public Realm Improvement Fund, controlled by a Public Realm Improvement Fund Governing Group that consists of nine local government representatives. The group allocates funds for "public improvements" in Midtown East, consistent with a plan for incorporating public input. Anticipated improvements include public plazas, pocket parks, and subway entrances. Thus, the Midtown East rezoning presents a fairly direct land value capture opportunity—owners of TDRs received increased property rights under the law in exchange for returning some of that value to the city.

LVC OBSERVATION

By employing flexible TDR programs, municipalities can create and recover substantial new value or augment existing TDR programs with a land value capture component. By increasing the geographic transferability of TDRs in exchange for sharing in the sales price, cities can create substantial new public funds. Expanding the geographical area for potential receiving TDR sites increases the number of possible bidders for these allowances, likely raising the price. As the city usually takes a percentage of the price, the value captured for municipal use by the sale of the TDRs will increase. The city also could apply a multiplier to its FAR increase for TDR transfers, in which the city then recovers a portion of the receipts from the sale. Municipalities can institute a TDR program allowing for the transfer of building rights, with government sharing in the extra value that is generated. There is a win-win opportunity here.

Table 4.3

Estimated Land Value Capture Proceeds, New York City Midtown East, August 2017

Landmarked Building	Estimated TDR Sales Price for Building Owner	Estimated Amount of Land Value Captured by City
Grand Central Terminal	$368 million	$73 million
St. Patrick's Cathedral	$338 million	$67 million
Lever House	$104 million	$20 million
Central Synagogue	$61 million	$12 million

Source: Brenzel 2017

CHAPTER 5

Recommendations

The Dulles Airport Metrorail extension continues to raise funding from special assessments as the project moves through its much-delayed second phase. *Source: Tom Saunders/VDOT/Creative Commons*

Land value capture has aroused considerable interest as a way to fund construction and rehabilitation of needed urban infrastructure and other municipal programs. LVC tools require private landowners to return to the government those property value increases that result from governmental investment in improvements or changes in land use regulation. The evidence in this report points to various recommendations for policy makers, as outlined in this chapter.

Require Developers to Share the Cost of Infrastructure

Some LVC tools discussed in this report—exactions, impact fees, and linkage fees—ensure developers pay government for infrastructure or other public goods consumed by their work. These tools force developers to internalize the cost of infrastructure related to their projects by either building it themselves, contributing to a fund to expand municipal infrastructure, or supporting programs to meet demand or mitigate harms created by the new project. Municipalities should consider using these tools more often to privately fund public infrastructure and programs when possible. While they exist to support the needs of affected residents—not to bestow a new facility on all existing citizens—these tools can provide certain economies of scale that benefit a whole town. At minimum, they prevent developers from overconsuming existing resources.

Moreover, special assessments require landowners to reimburse government for improvements that benefit them specifically. Special assessments can be a powerful way to create value and thus revenue sources for new infrastructure. A government could build new improvements (such as a commuter rail station) and charge that cost to property owners within a certain radius who will use it, rather than spending general funds. This has been an effective means to expand streetcar transit in Portland, Seattle, and at San Francisco's Salesforce Transit Center (GAO 2010). Some major projects even use multiple special assessments to leverage additional funds, as was the case with the Los Angeles Metro Red Line and the Washington Metro Dulles Corridor Extension (GAO 2010). Municipalities might follow these examples, using special assessments to help fund future infrastructure projects and programs. A summary of LVC tools is found in table 5.1 (page 54).

Special assessment funding for public transit in Los Angeles, California, also enabled restoration of MacArthur Park in 1993.
Source: Metro Library and Archive/Flickr

Capture Value Created by Government Planning Initiatives and Investment

Policy makers should further explore LVC tools that capture some or all the increased values that result from government actions, including planning, legislative initiatives, and municipal changes. Governments have used LVC to recover land value increases in-kind following governmental initiatives, via incentive zoning with developer contributions of infrastructure, services, or cash and through transferable development rights with contributions to the municipality for increased transferability. These actions may increase density to achieve a policy goal, such as housing construction, and create additional value for landowners by granting extra rights or cost savings; LVC then returns a share of this value to the public through the required contribution or market mechanism.

Table 5.1

A Summary of Land Value Capture Tools

Tool	Operation	Examples	Advantages	Concerns
Exactions	Developer pays municipality via land dedication or in-lieu fee	Developer provides infrastructure or funding for a new project (e.g., roads, open space, or parks)	Requires the developer to internalize costs of needed infrastructure by providing necessary land or improvements	No added infrastructure for the rest of a community; potential constitutional limitations
Impact Fees	Developer pays municipality a one-time fee in exchange for the development's impact on municipal infrastructure	Developer pays for off-site infrastructure like schools or a water treatment plant	Prevents consumption of existing municipal resources by new development	No added infrastructure for rest of community; potential constitutional limitations
Linkage Fees	Municipality requires one-time payment of (usually) commercial developers to provide affordable housing elsewhere in town to mitigate the development's effects on housing demand and prices	Developer provides additional housing supply and resources	Adds to local affordable housing stock that otherwise would be consumed at market value as a result of developer's commercial project	May be especially vulnerable to "essential nexus" constitutional test, if link between commercial development and housing is insufficiently clear
Special Assessments	Municipality assesses fee on properties in limited area to pay for local improvements	Street lighting, commuter rail station, water and sewer lines	Longstanding use, legally accepted, payable over years (which can support bonds)	Restricted to limited areas; cannot benefit general community by definition
Incentive Zoning: Infrastructure	Developer provides infrastructure in exchange for zoning changes to allow increased building rights	City expands floor area ratio allowance; owner creates affordable housing or public spaces	Municipality gets bespoke infrastructure without expending public funds	Limited control over publicly available private spaces; consistency with planning goals
Incentive Zoning: Cash Contributions	Developer provides cash payments in exchange for zoning changes to allow increased building rights	City expands floor area ratio allowance; owner pays cash to city	Municipal receipts can fund programs anywhere in the city	Neighborhood bearing burden of increased building does not specifically benefit from the bonus; consistency with planning goals
Transferable Development Rights (TDRs)	Developer pays city a portion of sales price received for otherwise unused building rights for which the city has created extra flexibility	City creates new value in the land by increasing potential target lots for TDR transfer; owners pay a return from TDR sales price	City obtains cash used for infrastructure fund, supporting improvements without cash outlay	Planners must ensure that resulting density does not overburden receiving neighborhoods

Policy makers need to ensure that state enabling acts permit such local ordinances, or that they are amended to do so. Local laws appropriate to specific communities are also necessary. Some localities already have the seeds of land value creation programs, and these might be adapted to create additional value. For example, table 4.2 (page 49) shows sample TDR programs across the United States that support a variety of local goals, from agricultural preservation to sprawl reduction to senior housing provision. This type of legislation could be changed to grant developers extra TDR benefits in exchange for desired municipal contributions.

New LVC programs must align with the municipality's comprehensive plan and general planning goals. A program that sacrifices long-term viability for short-term gains is not desirable. With careful planning and foresight, however, a municipality can leverage high-value LVC programs to ensure lucrative new opportunities for both property owners and the town.

Reform Legal Rules

State law determines whether a particular LVC strategy is available to a municipality—whether it permits a specific LVC tool and whether that authorization allows for sophisticated land value capture. State enabling acts should grant local governments power to enact and impose LVC-related regulations. Local governments also typically need specific ordinances to operationalize these tools. California, for example, has state legislation creating the Southern California Rapid Transit District, but other states have only general special assessment legislation, or simply rely on common law principles. Municipalities will likely want to ensure that state laws adequately enable them to pass LVC ordinances that will ultimately provide modern infrastructure and programs, and fairly allocate the benefits and burdens of development.

New York City's 2017 expansion of the geographic transferability of TDRs in Midtown East added significant value to landmarked properties in the area, including St. Patrick's Cathedral (top), Lever House (center), and Central Synagogue (bottom). *Sources: OSTILL/ iStock/Getty Images Plus; Brookfield Properties; demerzel21/ iStock/Getty Images Plus*

Additionally, state and federal law would benefit from clarification. Of numerous possible examples, policy makers might consider:

- What is the distinction between an improvement's "local" and "general" benefits in the special assessment area?

- Where does a new park fit into "local" versus "general" benefits?

- How can policy makers reach decisions up front in such an ambiguous atmosphere, with only an ex post facto legal challenge to determine the answer?

- What rules should govern the operation and control of privately owned public spaces (POPS) created under incentive zoning, and who should set them?

All the LVC tools described in this report come with many legal unknowns, and that ambiguity complicates reliable and foresighted planning and policy making. Policy makers and citizens would benefit from legislation that clarifies important areas of the law, and corresponding courts could draw clearer lines.

Recognize and Plan for Constitutional Uncertainties

Since the 19th century, U.S. municipalities have used land value capture tools and viewed them as constitutionally permissible—especially special assessments. Other tools, such as transferable development rights, have only been deployed and upheld more recently. Judicial guidelines for permissible LVC programs, moreover, are by their nature amorphous. The constitutional issue usually revolves around one of two questions: First, did a regulatory taking occur? In other words, did the regulation "go too far," reducing an owner's property rights enough to require compensation? Second, was an exaction improper due to an insufficient "nexus" relationship or

"proportionality" between the government's demand from an owner and the harm that the owner's action has created? Policy makers should carefully analyze proposed actions, provide careful documentation to support their decisions, and work closely with legal counsel to avoid running afoul of current constitutional limitations.

Since the 19th century, U.S. municipalities have used land value capture tools and viewed them as constitutionally permissible—especially special assessments. Other tools, such as transferable development rights, have only been deployed and upheld more recently.

Moreover, two potential issues could further constrain policy decisions that depend on potential Supreme Court guidance. First, the Court has extended its scrutiny of exactions to in-lieu exaction fees, so it could expressly apply that reasoning to other charges such as impact fees and linkage fees. While some already believe these rulings may apply to other fees, a new, direct decision would clarify the issue. Second, the Court has so far applied its exaction rules only to adjudicative decisions—that is, where administrative-type bodies were determining in specific cases whether to grant permits or permissions to owners. It could therefore extend the nexus and proportionality standards to legislative decisions, which would mandate that ordinances setting fees clearly connect the cost of development and the fee, among other requirements, and such an extension would diminish the courts' usual deference to legislative determinations. To prevent a future overruling by courts, local legislatures would thus be wise to consider making those clear connections and formal findings in all new legislation.

Build Consensus, Defuse the Rhetoric

The topic of land value capture in the United States has long been debated by policy makers, citizens, and theorists. At times, the discussions have been sharp, with conflict between those resisting perceived intrusions into individual property rights and those seeking a greater return for the public through increased value capture by municipalities. This is not surprising, given the fundamental economic, social, and constitutional values at stake.

Sometimes, however, the heat of that rhetoric obscures certain fundamental truths. First, various LVC tools have been utilized in the United States and upheld within the legal system for generations. Second, the tools described in this report are generally consistent with the Fifth Amendment to the U.S. Constitution, if policy makers follow the guidelines set down by the courts. Proposals that "go too far," like a blanket rejection of all building rights, are likely to fail. But there is nonetheless sufficient room to institute LVC well within constitutional limits, based on policies of fairness and efficiency.

The U.S. Supreme Court has generally found land value capture tools to be consistent with the Fifth Amendment to the U.S. Constitution, provided policy makers follow guidelines of fairness, efficiency, and relevance. *Source: sharrocks/iStock/Getty Images Plus*

References

Alterman, Rachelle. 2012. "Land Use Regulations and Property Values: The 'Windfalls Capture' Idea Revisited." In *Oxford Handbook on Urban Economics and Planning*. eds. Nancy Brooks, Kieran Donanghy, and Gerrit-Jan Knapp, 755–786. Oxford, England: Oxford University Press.

(APTA) American Public Transportation Association. 2019. "The Real Estate Mantra—Locate Near Public Transportation." (October). https://www.apta.com/wp-content/uploads/The-Real-Estate-Mantra-Locate-Near-Public-Transportation.pdf

American Society of Civil Engineers. 2021. "Report Card for America's Infrastructure." 6–7.

Anuta, Joe. 2018. "JPMorgan Files for Air-Rights Transfer to Boost Midtown East Tower." *Crain's*. September 24.

Angstman v. City of Boise, 917 P.2d 409 (Idaho App. 1996).

Arizona Revised Statutes Annotated § 9-461.16.

Arlington County, Virginia, Zoning Ordinance § 15.5.8. 2005. https://arlingtonva.s3.amazonaws.com/wp-content/uploads/sites/38/2019/10/ACZO.pdf

Auerbach, Alan J., William G. Gayles, Byron Lutz, and Louise Sheiner. 2020. "Fiscal Effects of COVID-19." *Brookings Papers on Economic Activity*. September 23. https://www.brookings.edu/bpea-articles/fiscal-effects-of-covid-19/

Bartholomew, Keith, and Reid Ewing. 2011. "Hedonic Price Effects of Pedestrian- and Transit-Oriented Development." *Journal of Planning Literature* 26(1): 18–34.

Basch, Michelle. 2022. "Phase 2 of Metro's Silver Line Delayed Again." *WTOP News*, March 3, https://wtop.com/tracking-metro-24-7/2022/03/delayed-again-the-opening-of-phase-2-of-metros-silver-line

Been, Vicki. 2005. "Impact Fees and Housing Affordability." *Cityscape* 8(1): 139–185.

Been, Vicki. 1991. "'Exit' as a Constraint on Land Use Exactions: Rethinking the Unconstitutional Conditions Doctrine." *Columbia Law Review* 91(3): 473–545.

Been, Vicki, Ingrid Gould Ellen, and Katherine O'Regan. 2019. "Supply Skepticism: Housing Supply and Affordability." *Housing Policy Debate* 29(1): 25–40.

Blint-Welsh, Tyler, and Katie Honan. 2020. "New York Neighborhoods Fight New Housing, Each for Different Reasons." *Wall Street Journal*, January 28.

Bliss, Laura. 2019. "Oregon's Single-Family Zoning Ban Was a 'Long Time Coming.'" *CityLab*. July 2. https://www.citylab.com/equity/2019/07/oregon-single-family-zoning-reform-yimby-affordable-housing/593137

Board of Supervisors v. DeGroff Enterprises, Inc., 198 S.E.2d 600 (Virginia Supreme Court 1973).

Brenzel, Kathryn. 2017. "Analysis: Here's What Midtown East Landlords Could Make from Air Rights Sales." *The Real Deal*. August 2. https://therealdeal.com/2017/08/02/analysis-heres-what-midtown-east-landlords-could-make-from-air-rights-sales

_____. 2018. "JPMorgan Buys 667K SF of Air Rights from Grand Central for 2270 Park." *The Real Deal*. December 13. https://therealdeal.com/2018/12/13/jpmorgan-buys-667k-sf-of-air-rights-from-grand-central-for-270-park

Budds, Diana. 2020. "Will Upzoning Neighborhoods Make Homes More Affordable?" *Curbed*. January 30. https://www.curbed.com/2020/1/30/21115351/upzoning-definition-affordable-housing-gentrification

Calavita, Nico. 2015. "Value Capture and Community Benefits." *Zoning Practice* 32(6).

Calavita, Nico, and Alan Mallach. 2009. "Inclusionary Housing, Incentives, and Land Value Recapture." *Land Lines* (January): 15–21.

California Building Industry Association v. City of San Jose, 351 P.3d 974 (California Supreme Court 2015).

California State Legislature, Senate Governance and Finance Committee. 2011. "Assessing the Benefits of Benefit Assessments: A Guide to Benefit Assessments in California." (September). https://sgf.senate.ca.gov/sites/sgf.senate.ca.gov/files/Assessing%20the%20Benefits%20of%20Benefit%20Assessments%20801-S.pdf

Callies, David L., and Charles L. Siemon. 1976. "The Value Capture Hypothesis: A Second Analysis." *Transportation Law Journal* 8(1): 9–45.

Callies, David L., and Christopher J. Duerksen. 1974. "Value Recapture as a Source of Funds to Finance Public Projects." *Urban Law Annual* 8: 73–95.

Carozzi, Felipe, Sandro Provenzano, and Sefi Roth. 2020. "Urban Density and COVID-19." IZA Institute of Labor Economics. IZA-DP-No. 13440 (July). ftp.iza.org/dp13440.pdf

Chapman, Jeffrey. 2017. "Value Capture Taxation as an Infrastructure Funding Technique." *Public Works Management and Policy* 22(1): 31–37.

Chen, Hong, Anthony Rufolo, and Kenneth Dueker. 1998. "Measuring the Impact of Light Rail Systems on Single Family Home Values: A Hedonic Approach with GIS Application." *Transportation Research Record: Journal of the Transportation Research Board* 1617 (1): 38–43.

Churchill, Winston. "Land and Income Taxes in the Budget [17 July 1909]." 1909. In *Liberalism and the Social Problem*. https://www.gutenberg.org/files/18419/18419-h/18419-h.htm#LAND_AND_INCOME

City of Chicago, Department of Planning and Development. 2020. "City Council Approves High Cap Funding & Reforms to the Neighborhood Opportunity Fund Program." February 19. https://www.chicago.gov/city/en/depts/dcd/provdrs/ec_dev/news/2020/january/higher-funding-cap-proposed-for-nof-new-construction-grants.html

City of Chicago. 2018. "Neighborhood Opportunity Bonus: 2017 Annual Financial Report." (Summer). https://www.chicago.gov/content/dam/city/depts/zlup/Planning_and_Policy/Publications/NOB_Annual_Report_2017_Final.pdf

Colorado Revised Statute Annotated § 30-28-401.

Connecticut General Statutes Annotated § 8-2g.

David, Greg. 2022. "Midtown Office-to-Apartment Conversion Gains Hochul and Adams Support." *The City*. March 7. https://www.thecity.nyc/manhattan/2022/3/7/22966532/midtown-office-apartment-conversion-hochul-adams

Della Rocca, Michael, Tyler Duvall, and Rob Palter. 2017. "The Road to Renewal: How to Rebuild America's Infrastructure." McKinsey & Co. (March). https://www.mckinsey.com/industries/travel-logistics-and-infrastructure/our-insights/the-road-to-renewal-how-to-rebuild-americas-infrastructure

Dolan v. City of Tigard, 512 U.S. 374 (1994).

Elmendorf, Christopher S., and Darien Shanske. 2020. "Auctioning the Upzone." *Case Western Reserve Law Review* 70: 513–572.

Engquist, Erik. 2020. "Bushwick Rezoning Impasse Puts de Blasio's Housing Plan at Risk." *The Real Deal*, January 15. https://therealdeal.com/2020/01/15/bushwick-rezoning-impasse-puts-de-blasios-housing-plan-at-risk/

Evans-Cowley, Jennifer S., and Larry L. Lahon. 2003. "The Effects of Impact Fees on the Price of Housing and Land: A Literature Review." *Journal of Planning Literature* 17(3): 351–359.

Fainstein, Susan. 2012. "Land Value Capture and Justice." In *Value Capture and Land Policies*. eds. Gregory K. Ingram and Yu-Hung Hong, 21–40. Cambridge, MA: Lincoln Institute of Land Policy.

Fennell, Lee Anne. 2000. "Hard Bargains and Real Steals: Land Use Exactions Revisited." *Iowa Law Review* 86(1): 1–85.

Fischel, William A. 2015. *Zoning Rules! The Economics of Land Use Regulation*. Cambridge, MA: Lincoln Institute of Land Policy.

Florida Statutes § 125.01055, 170.01(3).

Freemark, Yonah. 2020. "Upzoning Chicago: Impacts of a Zoning Reform on Property Values and Housing Construction." *Urban Affairs* 56(3): 758–789.

Froelich, Carter T., and Lucy Gallo. 2014. "An Overview of Special Purpose Taxing Districts." Washington, DC: National Association of Home Builders (September).

(GAO) U.S. Government Accountability Office, "Public Transportation: Federal Role in Value Capture Strategies for Transit Is Limited, but Additional Guidance Could Help Clarify Policies." 2010. GAO-10-781. Washington, DC: U.S. Government Accountability Office.

Grabar, Henry. 2012. "A Matchmaker for New York's Privately Owned Public Spaces." *Bloomberg*. October, 23. https://www.citylab.com/design/2012/10/matchmaker-new-yorks-privately-owned-public-spaces/3646/

Hagman, Donald G., and Dean J. Misczynski (eds.). 1978. "Executive Summary." *Windfalls for Wipeouts: Land Value Capture and Compensation*. Chicago, IL: American Planning Association.

Hamidi, Shima, Sadegh Sabouri, and Reid Ewing. 2020. "Does Density Aggravate the COVID-19 Pandemic? Early Results and Lessons for Planners." *Journal of the American Planning Association* 86(4): 495–509.

Higgins, Christopher, and Pavlos Kanaroglou. 2016. "Forty Years of Modelling Rapid Transit's Uplift in North America: Moving Beyond the Tip of the Iceberg." *Transport Reviews* 36(5): 610–634.

Homsy, George C., Gina Abrams, and Valerie Monastra. 2015. "Incentive Zoning: Understanding a Market-Based Planning Tool." Binghamton University Public Administration Faculty. (June). https://orb.binghamton.edu/cgi/viewcontent.cgi?article=1000&context=public_admin_fac

House of Commons, Housing, Communities and Local Government Committee. 2018. "Land Value Capture." Tenth Report of Session 2017–19, HC 766. https://publications.parliament.uk/pa/cm201719/cmselect/cmcomloc/766/766.pdf

Huffman, Forrest, and Marc Smith. 1987. "The Economics of Linkage Fees." *University of Florida Journal of Law and Public Policy* 1(1): 45–54.

Iacono, Michael, David Levinson, Zhirong (Jerry) Zhao, and Adeel Lari. 2009. "Value Capture for Transportation Finance: Report to the Minnesota Legislature." The Center for Transportation Studies, University of Minnesota. (June). https://conservancy.umn.edu/bitstream/handle/11299/97658/CTS%2009-18S.pdf?sequence=1&isAllowed=y

Jacobus, Rick. 2015. *Inclusionary Housing: Creating and Maintaining Equitable Communities*. Policy Focus Report. Cambridge, MA: Lincoln Institute of Land Policy.

Jaeger, William K. 2006. "The Effects of Land-Use Regulations on Property Values." *Environmental Law* 36(1): 105–130.

Kane, Joseph W., and Adie Tomer. 2019. "Shifting into an Era of Repair: U.S. Infrastructure Spending Trends." Brookings Metropolitan Infrastructure Initiative. (May 10). https://www.brookings.edu/research/shifting-into-an-era-of-repair-us-infrastructure-spending-trends/

Kansas Statutes Annotated § 12-16, 120.

Kansas-Lincoln, L.C. v. Arlington County Board, 2004 WL 2850651 (Va. Cir. Ct. 2004).

Karl F. Seidman Consulting Services and Consult Econ, Inc. 2016. "*Linkage Nexus Study Final Report to Boston Planning and Development Agency*." (December).

Kayden, Jerold S. 2000. *Privately Owned Public Spaces: The New York City Experience*. New York, NY: Wiley.

Kim, Minjee. 2020a. "Negotiation or Schedule-Based? Examining the Strengths and Weaknesses of the Public Benefit Exaction Structures of Boston and Seattle." *Journal of the American Planning Association* 86(2): 208–221.

_____.2020b. "Upzoning and Value Capture: How U.S. Local Governments Use Land Use Regulation Power to Create and Capture Value from Real Estate Developments." *Land Use Policy*. 95(104624): 1–12.

Knox v. City of Orland, 4 Cal. 4th 132, 142 (1992).

Kober, Eric. 2020. "De Blasio's Mandatory Inclusionary Housing Program: What Is Wrong, and How to Make It Right." The Manhattan Institute. (January).

_____. 2018. "Uses and Abuses of Value Capture for Transit." NYU Wagner, Rudin Center for Transportation Policy and Management. (February).

Koontz v. St. Johns River Water Management District, 570 U.S. 595 (2013).

Levinson, David, and Emilia Istrate. 2011. "Access for Value: Financing Transportation Through Land Value Capture." Washington, DC: Metropolitan Policy Program at Brookings. (April).

Lindblom, Mike. 2009. "Streetcar Cost Overruns: What About the Next Line?" *Seattle Times*, December 24.

Lingle v. Chevron, 544 U.S. 528 (2005).

Los Angeles Zoning Code § 14.5.1–14.5.12.

Mandelker, Daniel R. 2016. "Spot Zoning: New Ideas for an Old Problem." *Urban Lawyer* 48(4): 737–783.

Maryland Land Use Code § 7-101(9), § 7-101–7-104.

Maryland Local Government Code § 21-103.

Massachusetts General Laws, chapter 40A, § 9.

Mazur, Christopher. 2019. "For Renters, Housing Cost Burden Is About the Same." United States Census Bureau. November 4. https://www.census.gov/library/stories/2019/11/decade-after-the-recession-housing-costs-ease-for-homeowner.html

Menomonee Falls, Wisconsin, Code of Ordinances, § 86-12(c).

Michigan Statutes § 41.725.

Minnesota Statutes § 435.193.

McCarthy, George W. 2017. "Values and Land Value Capture." *Land Lines* (April): 2–4.

McCubbins, Matthew D., and Ellen C. Seljan. 2020. "Fiscal Secession: An Analysis of Special Assessment Financing in California." *Urban Affairs Review* 56(2): 480–512.

Melnick, Marc N. 1993. "New Avenues for Special Assessment Financing." *Urban Lawyer* 25(3): 539–565.

Merriman, David. 2018. *Improving Tax Increment Financing (TIF) for Economic Development*. Policy Focus Report. Cambridge, MA: Lincoln Institute of Land Policy.

Misczynski, Dean J. 2012. "Special Assessment in California: 35 Years of Expansion and Restriction." In *Value Capture and Land Policies*. eds. Gregory K. Ingram and Yu-Hung Hong, 97–115. Cambridge, MA: Lincoln Institute of Land Policy.

Montgomery County v. Woodward & Lothrop, Inc., 376 A.2d 483 (Md. 1977).

Mullen, Clancy, and Duncan Associates. 2019a. "Impact Fees Since the Recession." Paper presented at annual Growth and Infrastructure Consortium conference, Atlanta (October 24).

_____. 2019b. ImpactFees.com "National Impact Fee Survey: 2019." www.impactfees.com/publications%20pdf/2019survey.pdf

Murr v. Wisconsin, 137 S. Ct. 1933 (2017).

National Low Income Housing Coalition. 2020. "Census Bureau Releases Data from 2019." September 28. https://nlihc.org/resource/census-bureau-releases-data-2019-acs

New York City, Department of City Planning. "Privately Owned Public Space Current Standards." https://www1.nyc.gov/site/planning/plans/pops/pops-plaza-standards.page

New York City, Office of the Comptroller. 2017. "Audit Report on the City's Oversight Over Privately Owned Public Spaces." Report SR16-102A. April 18. https://comptroller.nyc.gov/wp-content/uploads/documents/SR16_102A.pdf

New York City Zoning Resolution §§ 37-70, 74-76, 74-634, 81-60 to 81-66.

New York General City Law § 81-d.

Newport Partners, LLC and Virginia Polytechnic Institute and State University. 2008. *Impact Fees and Housing Affordability: A Guidebook for Practitioners*. Washington, DC: U.S. Department of Housing and Urban Development, Office of Policy Development and Research.

Nichols, Chrissy Mancini. 2012. "Value Capture Case Studies: Washington DC Metro Expansion to Dulles Airport." Metropolitan Planning Council. (April 12). https://www.metroplanning.org/news/6384/Value-Capture-Case-Studies-Washington-DC-Metro-expansion-to-Dulles-Airport

Nichols, Chrissy Mancini. 2015. "Value Capture Remains Important Transit Financing Tool." Metropolitan Planning Council. (June 15). https://www.metroplanning.org/news/7159/Value-capture-remains-important-transit-financing-tool

Nollan v. California Coastal Commission, 483 U.S. 825 (1987).

Northern Virginia Affordable Housing Alliance. Undated. "Commercial Linkage Fees in Northern Virginia: A Primer." https://nvaha.org/wp-content/uploads/2014/11/NVAH_1311_CommImpactRpt-WEB.pdf

Oregon House Committee on Human Services and Housing, 80th Legislative Assembly. 2019. "Oregon Bill Summary, 2019 Regular Session, House Bill 2001." (April 8).

Oregon Revised Statutes § 197.758.

Pagano, Michael A., and Christopher W. Hoene. 2018. "City Budgets in An Era of Increased Uncertainty: Understanding the Fiscal Policy Space of Cities." Washington, DC: Metropolitan Policy Program at Brookings. (July).

Penn Central Transportation Company v. New York City, 438 U.S. 104 (1978).

Pennsylvania Coal Co. v. Mahon, 260 U.S. 393 (1922).

Placek, Christopher. 2020. "Impact Fee for Teardowns Proposed in Arlington Heights." *Daily Herald*, January 14. https://www.dailyherald.com/business/20200114/impact-fee-for-teardowns-proposed-in-arlington-heights

Reina, Vincent J. 2019. "Affordable Housing, But for How Long? The Opportunity and Challenge of Mandating Permanently Affordable Housing." *Fordham Urban Law Journal* 46(5): 1267–1294.

Rosenberg, Eli. 2017. "A 'Members Only' Public Space in Manhattan? Join the Club," *New York Times*. April 20. https://www.nytimes.com/2017/04/19/nyregion/public-space-trump-tower.html

Rossi, Jim, and Christopher Serkin. 2019. "Energy Exactions." *Cornell Law Review* 104(3): 643–713.

San Remo Hotel, L.P. v. San Francisco, 41 P.3d 87 (California Supreme Court 2002).

Schuetz, Jenny, Rachel Meltzer, and Vicki Been. 2009. "31 Flavors of Inclusionary Zoning: Comparing Policies from San Francisco, Washington, DC, and Suburban Boston. *Journal of the American Planning Association* 75(4): 441–456.

(Seattle) Office of Policy and Management, City of Seattle. 2005. "South Lake Union Streetcar, Capital Financing and Operating Maintenance Plan." (April 13). http://ctod.org/pdfs/2005SouthLakeUnionStreetcarFinancing.pdf

Shishir, Mathur. 2019. "Value Capture to Fund Public Transportation: The Impact of Warm Springs BART Station on the Value of Neighboring Residential Properties in Fremont, CA." Mineta Transportation Institute Publications, San Jose Institute. 37–38. https://scholarworks.sjsu.edu/cgi/viewcontent.cgi?article=1265&context=mti_publications

Solvang Municipal Improvement District v. Board of Supervisors, 112 Cal. App.3d 545, 552-553 (1980).

Small, Eddie. 2019. "City Council Give Green Light for JPMorgan's New Headquarters in Midtown East." *The Real Deal*, May 8.

Smith, Jeffrey J., and Thomas A. Gihring. 2006. "Financing Transit Systems Through Value Capture: An Annotated Bibliography." *The American Journal of Economics and Sociology* 65(3): 751–786.

Smolka, Martim O. 2013. *Implementing Value Capture in Latin America: Policies and Tools for Urban Development*. Policy Focus Report. Cambridge, MA: Lincoln Institute of Land Policy.

Southern Burlington County NAACP v. Mt. Laurel, 456 A.2d 390 (New Jersey Supreme Court 1983).

Spielman, Fran. 2020. "Fran Spielman, Lightfoot Alters Rahm Emanuel's Neighborhood Opportunity Fund to Make it Her Own." *Chicago Sun Times*. January 21. https://chicago.suntimes.com/city-hall/2020/1/21/21075457/lightfoot-alters-rahm-emanuels-neighborhood-opportunity-fund-make-it-her-own

Sprunt, Barbara. 2021. "Biden Says Final Passage of $1 Trillion Infrastructure Is Big Step Forward." NPR. November 6. https://www.npr.org/2021/11/05/1050012853/the-house-has-passed-the-1-trillion-infrastructure-plan-sending-it-to-bidens-des

Stromberg, Brian, and Lisa Sturtevant. 2016. "What Makes Inclusionary Zoning Happen?" *National Housing Conference*. (May). https://nhc.org/wp-content/uploads/2017/10/What-makes-inclusionary-zoning-happen.pdf

Surico, John. 2019. "The Many Ways to Fund New York City's Big Subway Fix." *City Lab*. January 2. https://www.citylab.com/transportation/2019/01/fix-new-york-city-subway-mta-funding-congestion-pricing/579262/

Tagtachian, Daniela A., Natalie N. Barefoot, and Adrienne L. Harreveld. 2019. "Building by Right: Social Equity Implications of Transitioning to Form-Based Codes." *Journal of Affordable Housing and Community Development Law* 28(1): 71–115.

Town of Telluride v. Lot Thirty-Four Venture, 3 P.3d 30 (Colorado Supreme Court 2000).

Tennessee Code § 66-35-102.

Texas Local Government Code, title 7, § 214.905.

Thaden, Emily, and Ruoniu Wang. 2017. "Inclusionary Housing in the United States: Prevalence, Impact, and Practices." Working paper. Cambridge, MA: Lincoln Institute of Land Policy. https://www.lincolninst.edu/sites/default/files/pubfiles/thaden_wp17et1_0.pdf

U.S. Census Bureau. 2017a. "Table 1: State and Local Govt. Finances by Level of Government and by State: 2017." *2017 State and Local Govt. Finance, Historical Datasets and Tables*. https://www.census.gov/data/datasets/2017/econ/local/public-use-datasets.html

_____. 2017b. Population of Interest, Criteria for Classifying Governments. https://www.census.gov/programs-surveys/gus/technical-documentation/methodology/population-of-interest1.html. and Table 4: Special Purpose Local Governments by State. https://www.census.gov/data/tables/2017/econ/gus/2017-governments.html

_____. 2006. Census Classification Manual. p. 4-38, 6-10. https://www2.census.gov/govs/pubs/classification/2006_classification_manual.pdf

_____. 2018. American Community Survey: 2014–2018 ACS 5-Year Narrative Profile. https://www.census.gov/acs/www/data/data-tables-and-tools/narrative-profiles/2018/report.php?geotype=nation&usVal=us

Urban Institute. "State and Local Revenues." https://www.urban.org/policy-centers/cross-center-initiatives/state-and-local-finance-initiative/state-and-local-backgrounders/state-and-local-revenues#time

Virginia Code § 15.2-4802.

Walters, Lawrence C. 2013. "Land Value Capture in Policy and Practice." *Journal of Property Tax Assessment and Administration* 10(2): 5–21.

Walters, Lawrence C. 2012. "Are Property-Related Taxes Effective Value Capture Instruments?" In *Value Capture and Land Policies*. ed. Gregory K. Ingram and Yu-Hung Hong, 187–214. Cambridge, MA: Lincoln Institute of Land Policy.

Washington Revised Code §§ 35.43.070, 35.43.180, 35.43.210.

Whitford, Emma. 2016. "Inside the $220 Million Plan to Improve the Subway at Grand Central." *The Gothamist*, October 18. https://gothamist.com/news/inside-the-220-million-plan-to-improve-the-subway-at-grand-central

Whittemore, Andrew H. 2017. "Racial and Class Bias in Zoining: Rezonings Involving Heavy Commercial and Industrial Land Use in Durham (NC), 1945–2014." *Journal of the American Planning Association*. 83(3): 235–248.

Wisconsin Statutes Annotated § 66.1015(3).

Wolf-Powers, Laura. 2019. "Reclaim Value Capture for Equitable Urban Development." *Metropolitics*. (May 28). https://metropolitiques.eu/Reclaim-Value-Capture-for-Equitable-Urban-Development.html

Young, Bob. 2005. "Landowners Hop Aboard Lake Union Streetcar Line." *Seattle Times*, November 12, B1.

Youngman, Joan. 2016. *A Good Tax: Legal and Policy Issues for the Property Tax in the United States*. Cambridge, MA: Lincoln Institute of Land Policy

Acknowledgments

The author extends special thanks to Enrique Silva of the Lincoln Institute of Land Policy for his comments on this manuscript and general insights on land value capture. Thanks as well to the following Lincoln Institute colleagues for their helpful thoughts and exchanges over the years on value capture, land taxation, and municipal finance (in alphabetical order): Daphne Kenyon, Adam Langley, Semida Munteanu, Martim Smolka, and Joan Youngman. And thanks to George "Mac" McCarthy, President of the Lincoln Institute of Land Policy, for his encouragement and support in this exploration of land value capture.

Appreciation is also sent to the Lincoln Institute editorial and communications team for their comments and enhancements to this report, including (in alphabetical order) Allison Ehrich Bernstein, Maureen Clarke, Amy Finch, Will Jason, and Emily McKeigue.

Although the author is grateful for the assistance of these people, the work, opinions, and errors in this report are mine alone.

The 1994 Supreme Court case *Dolan v. City of Tigard* determined that a government agency cannot require landowners to surrender use rights without establishing a sufficiently "essential nexus"; in that case, the Dolans wished to expand their store without dedicating land to the public, as the city permit required. *Source: inversecondemnation.com*

ABOUT THE AUTHOR

Gerald Korngold is a professor of law at New York Law School and serves as a Distinguished Scholar at the Lincoln Institute of Land Policy in Cambridge, Massachusetts. Previously, he was dean of Case Western Reserve University School of Law (1997–2006). An elected member of the American Law Institute and the American College of Real Estate Lawyers, he has lectured nationally and internationally on land ownership and transactions, land use, and property law.

Professor Korngold writes and teaches in the fields of property, land use, and real estate law, including international property law. He authored *Private Land Use Arrangements*, now in its third edition; coauthored *Cases and Materials on Real Estate Transactions* with Paul Goldstein, now in its seventh edition; coauthored *Cases and Materials on Property* with Susan F. French, now in its seventh edition; and coedited *Property Stories* with Andrew Morriss, now in its second edition. He has also published numerous articles in law reviews and journals.